HILLTOP DOC

A Marine Corpsman Fighting Through
The Mud and Blood of the Korean War

SECOND EDITION

Leonard Adreon

© Copyright 2020 Leonard Adreon.

All rights reserved. No part of this publication may be reproduced, distributed, or transmitted in any form or by any means, including photocopying, recording, or other electronic or mechanical methods, without the prior written permission of the publisher, except in the case of brief quotations embodied in critical reviews and certain other noncommercial uses permitted by copyright law.

Photo credits: Military action photos are in the public domain, and are by the United States Marine Corps, with the following exceptions. Photo of the Chinese casualty in chapter 2 is from the U.S. Army Heritage and Education Center. Photos of bugler, old Korean man, and soldier with Korean child are by the Department of Defense. Photos of the United States Naval Training Station in Idaho, the class of Farragut trainees, the USS General M. C. Meigs, and the aerial photo of Naval Station Newport are by the U.S. Navy. Photo of Chinese running up a hill is by the Chinese Military Science Academy. Photos of the port at Pusan and soldiers at attention in the cemetery are by the U.S. Army. Photos of Sportsman's Park, Washington University, San Francisco, the Zippo lighter and the mountains are photos in the public domain. All other photos are the property of Leonard Adreon.

Library of Congress Control Number: 2016963009

ISBN: 978-1-950419-04-3 (print)
ISBN: 978-1-950419-05-0 (ebook)

Book design by LaVidaCo Communications

Printed in the United States of America

First printing edition 2017

"This book is a fascinating first-hand account from a Korean War veteran who remained silent for more than 60 years about his experiences. A personal account, but a story that will be appreciated by a wide audience of readers. I am thrilled that writing classes at Washington University inspired this author!"

– Chancellor Mark S. Wrighton,
Washington University

"I was inspired reading Hilltop Doc. As a former Marine machine gunner, I could feel the esprit de corps that flows through every engrossing combat chapter of this book."

– Richard (Rick) Glassman,
4th Marine Division, 1964-1970

Table of Contents

Poems   VII
Prologue   XI

CORPSMAN!

Chapter 1	They called us Doc	1
Chapter 2	Bugles and whistles	7
Chapter 3	The wounds of war	11
Chapter 4	Esprit de Corps	17
Chapter 5	Surreal survival	21
Chapter 6	Gotta pen?	27
Chapter 7	A deadly Dead Time	31
Chapter 8	Payback	39
Chapter 9	The bet	45
Chapter 10	Dodging mortars	51

PATHWAY TO WARS

Chapter 11	Direct hit	57
Chapter 12	Sink or swim	61
Chapter 13	P for Protestant	67
Chapter 14	The hill we lost	71
Chapter 15	Final duty WWII	77
Chapter 16	We paid too much	83
Chapter 17	My college years	89
Chapter 18	Big Mike remembers Iwo Jima	95
Chapter 19	My worst moment	99

SAILOR, CIVILIAN, MARINE

Chapter 20 The recall 105
Chapter 21 From swabby to Marine 109
Chapter 22 Steady hands 117
Chapter 23 My Pacific cruise 123
Chapter 24 A gift unexpected 127
Chapter 25 Last liberty 133
Chapter 26 Stench to stalemate 137
Chapter 27 Korean kindness 141
Chapter 28 City of orphans 145
Chapter 29 Trench trauma 149
Chapter 30 Dodging a bullet 155
Chapter 31 To the 38th 161

CONFUSION AND CONSEQUENCES

Chapter 32 Mistakes happen 169
Chapter 33 A blown trip to Seoul 175
Chapter 34 What took so long? 181
Chapter 35 Confusion in San Francisco 187
Chapter 36 Smoking kills 191
Chapter 37 Dilemma at Newport 197
Chapter 38 Final decision 201
Chapter 39 Invisible wounds 205
Chapter 40 The diary 211
Chapter 41 Vacationing home 217
Chapter 42 Another ending 221

HISTORY AND PERSPECTIVE

Epilogue 229
Poems 235
The story continues 245
Final observations 251
About the author 259

We Paid Too Much

Leonard Adreon

The cold is numbing, icy pellets fall,
The air dense with fog,
Visibility impaired. The Gooks can't see us,
The sergeant shouts, "Go," we start up the hill.

Gooey mud washes over us,
We claw and slither our way up,
Elbows propelling movement, weapons in front,
Flashes of light, shells screeching, hitting, exploding.

The earth shakes, a yell, "Marine down,"
face in the muck, roll him over,
stop the bleeding, morphine for pain,
There is blood, no bleeding, no pain.

We've seen it too much, the vacant stare,
Press the eyelids closed,
don't know why, we just do it,
A fellow Marine gone forever.

We reach the top, a jumble of bodies
left behind to cart away,
Lifeless faces of Chinese youth,
The ground red from the rain washed dead.

Two hundred and ten went up the hill,
Eighty Seven reached the top,
Another hill, another day,
We own the hill.

We paid too much.

Warrior Poet

Leonard Adreon

Washington U's Dean Mark Taylor
tagged me The Warrior Poet
of the Korean War
A dramatic title
A high compliment
It made me smile
Should I feel proud
I thought about it
Memories burst forth
Reality set in

The warrior is long gone
Only the poet remains

Six decades ago
The warrior was young
Quick brash feisty strong

The warrior fired his carbine
Bullets flew in rapid succession
Aimed at the faceless shadows
of enemy soldiers
dashing from gulley to gulley
I saw them fall, get up, crawl
fall again and lie still on cold earth

An enemy soldier rushed forward
eyes squinted with fierce intent
his weapon drawn and aimed
I grabbed my 45 pistol
fired 6 successive rounds
his body jolted and fell
back violently shaking
The shaking stopped

The battle ended
quiet descended
I scrambled up
to his lifeless body
wiped the black blood
from his sad face
His unseeing eyes
stared at me
I gently closed his eyelids
He was just a kid
just a teenage kid

It was at that moment
that the warrior faded away
The war went on
battle after battle
With no choice I killed again but

The warrior was gone.

Prologue

This is an expanded edition of my original memoir that focused on my Korean War combat experiences. It includes five new chapters, some of which were too difficult for me to write in 2017. I hope this new edition is a more comprehensive account of that intense war. It also includes a chapter with my opinions on the current dangerous situation in Korea.

My life was saved and forever changed on a scruffy hillside in Korea in 1951. Responsible for both was a man I hardly knew, a man called Big Mike, or Sarge or just Mike. He was about 6-foot-2-inches tall, with a square build, and, at least, a decade older than the rest of us.

Mike was rough looking, with a prominent nose that looked to have been broken a time or two, eyes of steely grey, and a face always unshaven. Not handsome in the classic sense, his looks exuded power.

We all liked Mike. At base camp, he took time to meet one-on-one with new replacements, usually kids 18-to-21-years old. He'd tell them about combat in the hills, ease their anxieties, say he'd be there for them. He offered advice on protecting themselves, keeping weapons ready, taking no unnecessary risks.

He knew that despite gung-ho facades, they were scared and uncertain. They listened as I had listened. Combat savvy, Mike was a survivor of Iwo Jima where he'd earned two purple hearts and a bronze star. We respected him.

I don't remember if he had family or where he was from. I don't remember his name beyond Mike. Mike was proud to be a Marine. He made the rest of us proud. I am grateful to a man who probably had no idea of the impact he had on others.

Later, I write more about that hill and that day, about how Big Mike saved our lives before he lost his.

I was in Korea for parts of 1951 and 1952, one among thousands of men and women serving there. I was told what to do and where to go. I was a Hospital Corpsman Third Class assigned to the First Marine Division.

In fact, in roughly three years of active duty, I didn't advance beyond my starting rank of petty officer, third class. Not impressive. I had progressed faster in the Boy Scouts. That all contributed to my doubts that anyone would want to hear or read what I had to say.

I didn't discuss my experiences in Korea for 60 years. I didn't talk about Korea with my mom, dad or my brother. I told them I wanted to avoid the subject, and they seemed content I was home and uninjured.

I met my wife, Audrey, in 1953, not long after I'd returned. She knew I'd been in Korea but understood I wanted to put

Prologue

it behind me. Not once in those six decades did we discuss the war.

My silence broke in 2011, after I enrolled in Washington University writing classes through a program called Lifelong Learning. Students and facilitators encouraged me to write about the war and my role. I hesitated, and then penned a short poem about taking a hill. I read it to a gathering of students and a friend, Dick Hyde, asked me to talk with a class he was facilitating on the Korean War.

The class surprised me with their interest in what happened at the 38th Parallel. My crisp memory also surprised me. People at the university strongly urged me to write about the realities of combat. They thought too many young people think of war in the heroic terms depicted in movies. To me, war is anything but heroic. It is brutal and ugly, full of blood, mud, death and pain.

So this is the story of an unsophisticated, 17-year-old kid drafted into the Navy in 1944 in the latter days of World War II. Before the draft, I had not traveled beyond St. Louis. I'd grown up in a family that struggled during the Great Depression.

My World War II service took me to Naval Station Great Lakes near Chicago, Illinois, to Farragut, Idaho and then to Evanston, Illinois. I followed that relatively uneventful phase with four years in college before being recalled to active duty in 1950. I went back to Naval Station Great Lakes, to Oceanside, California (Camp Pendleton) and to Korea. I finished my service in Newport, Rhode Island.

Leonard Adreon

This book focuses on my experience in the Korean War. It is about brave men and stark moments that changed many of us. Such as how Mike and that hill changed me. I cannot pinpoint exactly how. I knew it when I came back that day, and know it now.

I didn't talk about Korea for decades. But my experience there has lived with me every day.

Corpsman!

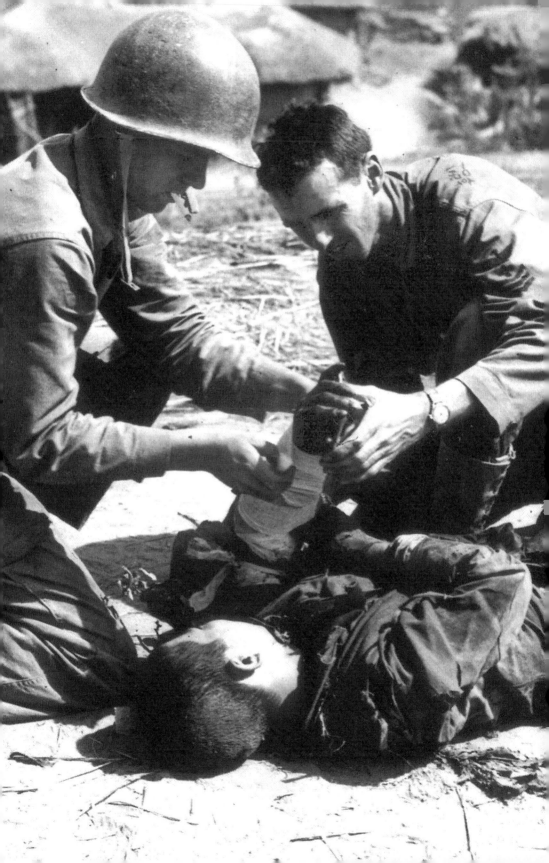

1

They called us Doc
Korea, 1951

About halfway to the top of the hill I heard my first yell of "Corpsman!" Some 20 yards ahead, I could see a Marine kneeling and waving his arms. I ran over and he pointed to his corporal lying in a small ditch. The wounded man screamed in pain as he rolled side to side, gripping his midsection. I took out my scissors, cut away his jacket and shirt, and pulled up his undershirt so I could see the wound. I had to pull his hands away to find blood oozing from his stomach.

To calm him, I injected morphine into his arm and grabbed some bandages, pressing them firmly against the wound. The injured man quieted somewhat. I asked his buddy to continue pressing the bandages until the blood stopped flowing.

It was the first time I treated a wounded Marine on a hillside and I was trembling, sweat dripping from my forehead into my eyes and off my nose. I was unsure I did the right thing.

I took the Marine's M1 rifle and jabbed the bayonet into the ground, placing his helmet atop the rifle. That signaled stretcher teams that a wounded man needed transport. I filled out an EMT (emergency medical tag) that spelled out the treatment I'd given, hoping that would help those at the forward aid station know what was needed. I had learned all this six long years earlier and thousands of miles away.

My remarkable transformation to battlefield lifesaver was for real, though hardly complete. How this green corpsman had landed in the middle of the bloody Korean conflict was a startling tale of youthful negligence, military bumbling and bad luck.

I'd been drafted during World War II, something we all understood in the middle of what was a worldwide conflict between good and evil. Then I was assigned to the Navy and made a corpsman in a process as mysterious as it was high handed, coming on orders out of the blue that sent me traveling. I finished the corpsman training not long before the world war ended and before I could do much in it.

College filled the following years, an education that had nothing to do with wounds.

Now I found myself on that hill, six years after my limited medical training, shaking from my first encounter with a blood-soaked Marine. It never got easy the many times it happened in the months to come. But the shaking subsided as the reality sunk in: The heat of assault left no time to dwell on the trauma.

We'd felt fortunate that day, my first day in battle, because the sun was shining and the Marine Corsair planes could fly and pound the entrenched enemy. Prop-driven planes, the Corsairs carried 500-pound bombs, .50-caliber machine guns and 20-millimeter cannons. They often decided an assault's outcome.

When we attacked the hill, fire teams of four men alternated as they slowly started to climb, followed by the rest of the platoon. We would run maybe 30 or 40 yards in a crouched position, then hit the ground as the next group leap-frogged past.

A third of the way up the hill, the Chinese had opened fire with their guns and lobbed mortar shells. Smoke from the explosions filled the air like a dense fog. We fired at flashes above us, holding ourselves in a prone position as much as possible. The crescendo of noise made it harder and harder to hear orders from the sergeants and lieutenants leading the assault.

The Chinese held the hill with machine guns placed 50-to-100 yards from the top. Our steady climb paused until our heavier firepower could take out those guns. Shoulder-mounted bazookas fired a small, powerful rocket that blasted the barricaded machine-gun nests. We'd also throw hand grenades when we got close enough.

The Marines didn't expect corpsmen to fight, and didn't issue us grenades. But I often did fight and, because I could throw farther than some of the Marines, my buddies gave me grenades. I took pride in watching a grenade explode, silencing the rapid fire of a machine gun coming from an enemy bunker. On subsequent assaults, I was able to arm myself with grenades.

The deadly jets of blazing fuel from flame throwers also forced the enemy from machine-gun nests. A horrible scene would follow as a Chinese machine gunner ran out, his body on fire and his face black, the air filling with the smell of burning flesh.

My job was to treat the wounded and tag them. Stretcher teams followed, hauling the wounded to a med tent down the hill. We used small, brown WIA (Wounded in Action) or the emergency medical tags to identify the wound and what we'd done. This helped guide doctors at the hill's bottom to the best follow-up treatment.

Stretchers retrieved the untagged bodies, Marines who had died, only after the wounded had been moved off the hill. They eventually were tagged KIA (Killed in Action).

Frantic conditions meant the process often didn't go smoothly. Corpsman couldn't do much in the field beyond stemming bleeding and controlling pain with morphine. We might immobilize a broken arm or leg with splints made from pine branches or other wood we'd find. Our medkits carried the bare essentials for those ripped by shells or shrapnel.

Two medkits, each called Unit One, hung from my belt or across my shoulder. One contained scissors to cut away clothing, syrettes of morphine, an early antibiotic powder called sulfa, tubes of iodine, Merthiolate and alcohol. The other contained tourniquets, three sizes of bandages, gauze, medical tape, and a minor surgical kit consisting of a scalpel, suture threads, needles and hemostats for clamping arteries or veins. In warm weather we carried Chloroquine tablets given once a week for malaria. At times we used DDT spray for lice.

I'd arrived in Korea just days earlier, feeling unprepared with my meager medical training that now was years stale. I landed on the peninsula nervous, uncertain and concerned. Many other corpsmen later told me they shared that sense of inadequacy. But we also understood we were the frontline of care, and were all the Marines had in battle.

That became clear on that first of many hills. I'll never forget how that first wounded Marine I treated, whose name I never knew, looked up at me through the blood and, despite his misery and pain, mouthed the words, "Thank you, Doc."

That's what the Marines often called us, the ill-prepared and nervous corpsmen: They called us Doc.

2

Bugles and whistles
Korea, 1951

That night, like so many to come, would be filled with the sound of distant bugles and whistles.

We'd won the day. But a brutal scene met me when I got to the top of that first hill. Bodies of dead and wounded Chinese lay strewn around as the CCF (Chinese Communist Forces), unlike the Marines, left behind their dead and wounded.

The fixed stare on the young Chinese faces has stayed with me since. Most looked like high schoolers. We did our best to treat the Chinese wounded but had to be spare with our morphine so we wouldn't run out.

Communication with the enemy wounded was difficult. The only word we usually could exchange was "OK." So a young soldier surprised me. I was putting a splint on his broken leg when he spoke to me in broken English. His comrades had left him behind because he couldn't walk.

His sad hurt eyes looked up at me as he asked, "Will I be OK? Will someone tell my mother and father that I am OK?" I said I thought he would heal. I brought a small smile to his face when I said he could probably write his parents once treated at the POW camp.

We cleared the top and reshaped foxholes to fit our needs. Then we piled the dead Chinese and helped prepare their wounded so our stretcher guys could take them down the hill.

On the hill's north side, we set up machine gun nests to help repel a counterattack. Our entire company had scattered across the high ground. We used foxholes and trenches already there and dug others. We all needed a place in a foxhole or behind a barricade to escape shrapnel from the mortar fire we knew would come. Unlike the Marines, the Chinese usually attacked at night.

A pitch-black sky covered us that night as we maintained complete silence. About half slept in our sleeping bags while the others kept watch. Called mummy bags, they had added insulation to keep us warm in the winter or less padding to be lighter in the summer. A panic zipper on the bags enabled us to get out fast.

We slept fully clothed with our boots on, our weapons loaded on safety and our knives and bayonets available. We remained on constant alert because the Chinese would infiltrate the hilltop in small groups or individually and try to surprise a foxhole. They were well trained in using their deadly automatic weapons.

Between shells exploding came periods of quiet, broken only by the eerie sound of bugles and whistles coming from below. I found the sound intimidating and assumed that was its purpose, but later learned that's how the Chinese communicated with each other at night.

Whenever a Marine was hit and I heard, "Corpsman!," my job was to leave my foxhole and get to the wounded Marine as fast as I could. Still, I would try to time my run between mortar shells. Night foxholes could be a corpsman's most dangerous post. On this hill, my first, I was fortunate to not have to leave my foxhole.

The Chinese did not mount a counterattack. Several days later, I was relieved to see our replacements come up the road. I felt extremely lucky every time I left the battle front, also called the MLR or Main Line of Resistance, which was strung along the 38th Parallel that once was and would again be the border between North and South Korea.

With our replacements in place, all of the men of my "D" company, better known as Dog Company, packed up and came down the hillside. Walking down the winding road was easy compared to leapfrogging our way up.

It helped, too, to know that we'd get roughly 10 days back at the battalion base. That meant 10 days of relative comfort. Not all relaxing, as I and the other corpsmen would also work in the battalion aid station. But it was relatively safe, a break until we'd get thrown at the next hill.

Farragut Naval Training Station, Idaho (U.S. Navy)

3

The wounds of war
Idaho, 1944

My medical training, as such it was, came after the longest train ride of my life. That trip ended in a beautiful, lush valley surrounded by grand mountains. It still surprises me that a naval base sat in the middle of Idaho.

Beautiful Coeur D'Alene Lake lay nearby. I saw no evidence, however, that the Navy used this picturesque natural body of water. I appreciated the Navy sending me to this resort setting, though I wasn't enthused about my assignment as a hospital corpsman.

Trainers issued each of us a blue-bound book, the "Handbook of the Hospital Corps," our training text.

The handbook included chapters on medicines, first aid, treatments of various diseases, injuries, blood and laboratory work and much more. This was different duty than the boot camp I had just finished, Instructors focused on injuries that occurred on Navy ships.

The training also covered the wounds of war. I didn't see the relevance of learning to treat gunshot or shrapnel wounds in battlefield conditions. Only later did I learn that the Navy met the medical needs of the Marine Corps. Navy doctors and corpsmen provided essential service to Marines in combat.

The import to my later life was lost to me.

I made good but temporary friends at Farragut Naval Training Station. We worked a reasonable, five-day week and escaped on liberty most weekends. We went to the city of Coeur d'Alene, a beautiful and pleasant place, but not for sailors looking for action.

Later weekends found us in Spokane with more to do. Not all bad—Spokane included Sunday brunch at an Episcopal church. The congregation invited servicemen to brunch, prepared by church members and spectacularly delicious. Much different than food at the naval base.

News painted a positive outlook for Europe. The allies landed in Normandy that June. It appeared they had Germany and Italy on the ropes. Hopes rose that allies had found a path to victory in Europe.

However, the war in the Pacific raged with no end in sight. Most of us expected to soon be joining ships in the Pacific theater.

The wounds of war

A nice family at the church took a liking to me and invited me to dine with them one Saturday night. I liked their daughter, Renee, a high school senior and a bundle of laughs. Her parents encouraged us to hang out together. We toured Spokane, went biking and canoeing, hiked mountain trails and generally enjoyed each other's company. After boot camp and the medical training I was ready for some relaxation and fun.

On our last weekend together I gave Renee my home address in St. Louis. I said I'd write when I reached my new assignment. I didn't know how mail worked on sea duty.

The weeks rolled by at the Farragut school. We earned diplomas and I received the rank of Hospital Corpsman Third Class. I hoped my assignment would take me to a ship—I was in the Navy, after all.

But my orders were to Northwestern University at Evanston, Illinois to work on decommissioning the Naval V-12 College Training program. The Navy had agreements with universities to school personnel in subjects essential to the war effort.

I packed up my sea bag and said a fond farewell to my friends, whose orders scattered them around the world. Mine would take me to a premier and safe assignment at a top university not far from my home in St. Louis.

Back on a train heading for Chicago, I left the beautiful valley and the view of the mountains, looking forward to a new kind of duty. I wrote to Renee thanking her and telling her of my new assignment.

I received a nice note from her parents wishing me luck

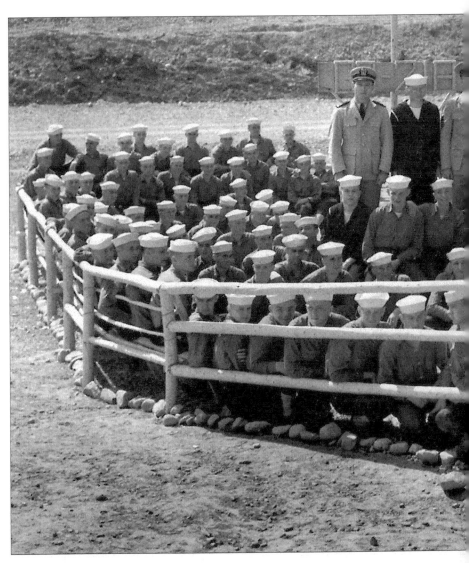

Trainees at Farragut base (U.S. Navy)

The wounds of war

and saying Renee was busy readying for her graduation. Goodbye, Idaho. Goodbye, Renee.

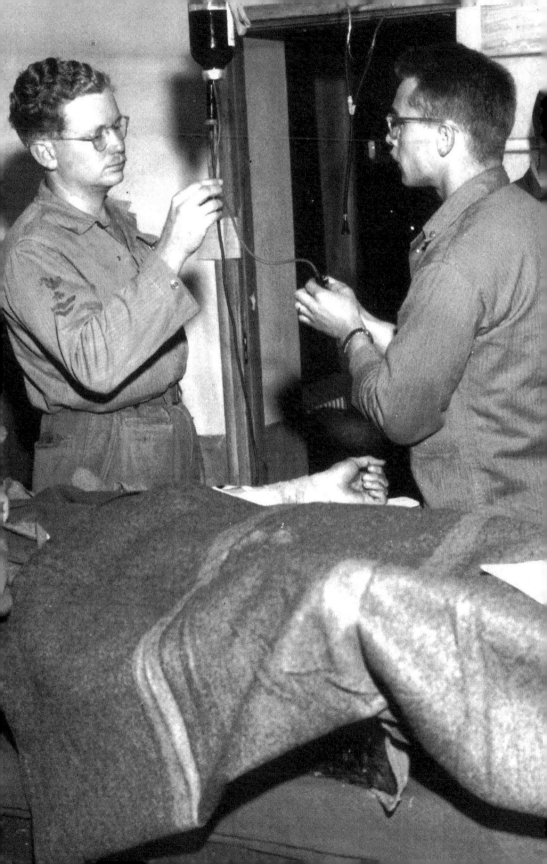

4

Esprit de Corps
Korea, 1951

When I got to Korea, I was just another replacement corpsmen. New replacements arrived every month.

But having landed in the middle of a strange peninsula, 7,000 miles from home, I expected a lot from myself. I knew the Marines did, too.

I was nervous. My medical training back in Farragut, Idaho was more than six years ago. My Handbook of the Hospital Corps nowhere to be found. The many notes taken in classes long gone.

During those years between, I took classes in economics, business, marketing and accounting. Hardly helpful for my Korean duties.

I'd had that brief duty at the end of WWII in the sickbay at Northwestern University. Its routines hardly prepared me for the battlefield.

My training at Camp Pendleton came to mind. A drill sergeant had pushed me to scale a wall, crawl under machine gun fire, climb uphill in sand, disassemble and reassemble my M1 carbine in the dark, fix a bayonet and to use the small serrated knife that came with it.

The drill sergeant did spend time on the role of the corpsman in supporting a platoon. I learned the weapons Marines would use, and was given the fundamentals of the bazooka, the M1 semi-automatic Garand rifle, grenades and the BAR, or Browning Automatic Rifle.

The sergeant talked about the importance of corpsmen in Korea. He credited a corpsman for treating him quickly when hit by shrapnel.

Fortunately, the doctors seemed eager to help us. They took time to show us how to treat the wounds we'd encounter. They even taught us how to remove pieces of shrapnel from a wound. The doctor I usually helped at the battalion aid station, who I knew as Doc Koz, was thorough with me and other corpsmen. It took a while, but after time with the doc, I felt better about my job.

Experienced corpsmen also shared their experience in handling what I would encounter. It was just a few months before I became one of them, a savvy guy helping green replacements back at base camp.

Esprit de Corps

Veteran Marines also helped train me. Some men had fought in World War II and knew about treating wounds. I soon took comfort in knowing how Marines helped each other, a spirit of "we are all in this together."

Each time I came back from the front at the 38th Parallel, I told the doctor about the wounded. He'd review what I'd done and make suggestions. He did so in a positive way, not as a criticism. His was the most beneficial training I got in Korea.

My landing in Korea came after the massive entry of the Chinese into the conflict. The Chinese entry came after a gamble, a miscalculation, by General MacArthur who convinced President Truman that the Chinese would not enter the war as they had threatened to do if US forces crossed the 38th Parallel. Their mistakes cost many lives. It also caused someone like me, recalled to active duty after many years, to arrive inadequately prepared.

Leadership screwed up. But the Marines, doctors, and fellow corpsmen watched out for each other. They readied me for the hillsides of Korea.

5

Surreal survival
Korea 1951

There was no time for introductions. Our platoon consisted of three squads, a total of 46 men. Since we were in this together, we quickly got to know each other.

Our lieutenant, who led the platoon, introduced me to the other platoon corpsman, a guy named Sammy. He told me that Sammy was experienced in the hill-by-hill warfare and could clue me in on what I needed to know.

I found Sammy to be friendly and helpful, even eager to help me understand what was needed and how to organize myself. One day, when things were quiet, we grabbed a beer at the rec tent, then went outside to sit on the ground for a chat.

Sammy, a quiet guy, didn't say much. But that day he opened up. Sammy was a Hospital Corpsman First Class, so he outranked me. He had been in Korea for several months, had climbed many hills and seen a lot of combat. He said, "Adreon, I am lucky to be talking to you today."

That began a startling conversation.

"Sammy, why do you say that?"

He smiled, "I'll tell you why, but only once." He explained that a couple of months after he arrived in Korea, with a

different platoon and different company, they took a smallish hill and secured their position. Everything seemed quiet as they dug in, set up defenses, and prepared for the night. "Then all hell broke loose."

I watched the color drain from his face. "It's OK if you don't want to talk about it," I said.

He sighed. "No, it might alert you to always be ready for what can come with the Chinese."

Sammy hesitated, then continued, "Don't know how it happened, but the Chinese surrounded us. A couple of hours before full darkness the Chinese attacked with a mortar barrage followed by hundreds of them coming as they fired their sub-machine burp guns. It was pure horror. We were not prepared. Outnumbered."

He took a deep breath, "The lieutenant ordered us to retreat off the hill as fast as we could. We were sitting ducks. The Chinese had filled the slope that we had come up blocking the path down. They mowed guys down as we tried to get off that hill. Marines dropped everywhere."

Sammy said he started toward the hill's edge, but could see he wasn't going to make it. "I didn't know what to do."

I shook my head and muttered, "Sammy, it sounds hopeless."

He shrugged, saying he pulled back from the hill's edge, stumbling over two dead Marines, one a big guy. The Chinese began to swarm the top of the hill. Sammy said he reached down, pushed the dead Marines aside, and crawled next to them.

"Then I pulled them over me. I played dead, concealed myself as much as I could. I'd tossed my med kits into a foxhole so the Chinese wouldn't spot me as a corpsman. Took off my watch and shoved it into my jacket pocket,"

"I just laid there barely breathing. A couple of their riflemen came by checking to make sure everyone was dead. They prodded the two dead Marines with the butts of their guns. Then, sure enough, one of them reached down and took the watch off the big guy and pried a ring off his finger. I held my breath until they walked away, careful not to move for what seemed like hours."

Sammy stood up. "This is too fuckin' hard; I don't want to talk about it anymore." He started to walk away.

"Wait, Sammy," I said. "How'd you get out of that?"

He sat back down, "Told ya' I was lucky. It was a black night. No moon, no stars. I lay there and listened for noise. Not a sound. The Chinese had shut down for the night."

He then described how he slowly and silently pushed the two Marines off and tossed his carbine aside. He described how he wiggled and squirmed to the edge of the hill. Nothing moved. He slid over the edge and down the hill. By daylight he reached the main service road and the forward med tent. "I pulled open the flap and fell into the first bunk I found."

Sammy shook his head several times, "Not proud of what I did. All those guys dead and I made it back by hiding."

No one asked him what happened. "My platoon and company destroyed. A few other guys made it back." He didn't ask them how.

Surreal Survival

He transferred to my company and platoon about two weeks later.

Sammy and I never again talked about his surreal survival.

6

Gotta pen?
Korea, 1951

Lives depended on us working together. Sammy and I, with the help of others, set up a forward aid tent adjacent to the main service road. Suddenly, shells whistled through the air. Officers ordered everyone to take shelter. We scattered into nearby woods.

Sammy and I crouched behind a giant boulder when a shell landed amid Marines clustered in a thicket of brush and trees. We rushed to help.

Our platoon corporal writhed on the ground, struggling to breathe. I couldn't find a wound, only that he was covered with debris and gasping. I yelled for Sammy to help me.

I was frantic. The Marine's face went pale, his body lurching and twisting on the ground. Sammy quickly recognized that his airway was blocked and shouted that the corporal needed a tracheotomy.

"Adreon, there's no time." Sammy said. "We must do it now."

Having heard of battlefield tracheotomies, I trembled, a cold sweat trickling down my face. "I've never done that. I was never trained to do it. I, I, I,-----"

"I can handle it," Sammy said. "Gotta pen?"

I found a pen in my back pocket. "OK, this'll work," he said.

The pen would hold open a hole that Sammy would cut into the Marine's throat, an emergency air passage. I knew what needed to be done. I wasn't ready to do it.

Sammy jarred me back to reality. "You better check the rest of the group," he said.

Breathing again myself, I ran into the woods looking for wounded Marines.

Back at the base, I asked Sammy about the corporal. He said he'd laid the Marine on his back with his neck extended, took his scalpel, cut a small vertical opening that he held open with the pen. It apparently worked—the Marine began breathing, though with difficulty.

Sammy sent a rifleman to find the doctor. The doctor removed the pen and inserted a tube to keep the airway open. Sammy probably saved his life.

I grew fairly comfortable giving first aid to our Marines. I never did feel confident I could cut an incision into someone's throat. I was relieved I didn't face that situation again.

Before my training at Farragut, Idaho and later at Pendleton I was even uncertain about taking blood, hooking

Gotta pen?

up an intravenous or even giving shots of Penicillin or morphine. Those treatments became routine.

I suspect most corpsmen felt the same. We had to help the wounded, keep them alive and do what we could for their survival.

But we lived with a constant fear. We knew a mistake could make things worse. We knew one might kill someone.

7

A deadly Dead Time
Korea, 1951

When I'd left the corpsman training school in Idaho, Renee's parents had sent me that gentle Dear John letter, letting me know their daughter was moving on.

That was better than the guys who got their Dear Johns in Korea, letters from sweethearts saying goodbye. For some, the breakup put them in a funk that interfered with their duties. Those times made me glad I'd gone to Korea with no girlfriend waiting back home.

Still, mail call was important for all of us, and came during our times back at the battalion station, away from the front. I got mail from my mom and dad and sometimes from my brother, Mert. I'd write them during down times at the battalion station, though I couldn't match the number of letters they sent. I tried to send a letter home every other week. I don't think I wrote anyone else and only a few letters to Mert. Years later, I looked for the letters to no avail.

I didn't write about combat. That meant I struggled to find something worth saying. Usually, I wrote about other guys and what we planned for when we came home. I'm sure the letters bored my family. I figured the important thing was for them to get something, even if it said nothing. All they really wanted was to know that I was OK.

Occasionally, but not often, their letters arrived with cookies or other goodies. When I told them that the cookies usually arrived smashed, they stopped sending them. The bubble gum they sent always arrived in good shape. Oddly, I enjoyed chewing and blowing bubbles. Maybe that was because I didn't smoke like most of the other guys. Cigarettes were plentiful and free.

I did most of my letter writing in the first couple of days back at the battalion station as we recovered from our time at the front. I'd also use that time to catch up on sleep.

These times were the cherished "Dead Times" between combat. Sometimes they stretched for a while. I have no idea why the conflict seemed to slow or even stop but we all welcomed the break. Oh, we patrolled to scout out the enemy, look for booby traps and check for mine fields. But all of us cherished the Dead Times.

To call interludes between deadly combat by that term seemed bizarre, but a lot of what happened in Korea seemed unexplainable.

A deadly Dead Time

We had the luxury of hot meals in the mess hall. Sitting on chairs at a table was a lot better than sitting on the ground eating C rations. Actually, I thought C rations were good. Most of the time we ate them cold, but sometimes we used Sterno and heated the cans. We had a lot of beans. My favorite was franks and beans. Also good was ham with Lima beans and just plain spaghetti. We also had canned peaches, packets of chocolate, graham crackers and cookies.

We'd also wash the crud from our clothes, repack our backpacks with clean gear, making sure we had a change of clothes, especially socks and underwear. I'd fill my two canteens with fresh water, though we also carried Halazone tablets to purify creek or pond water for drinking. Still, the dirty looking water seemed unsafe to drink, even after using the tablets.

I'd replenished my ammo. I always wanted two, thirty-round clips for my M1 carbine and after that first hill, carried several grenades on my belt. Later, I also carried a .45-caliber gun, so I needed its ammo on my bandolier. The bandolier mounted on shoulders with pockets for bullets.

Along with our carbine came a bayonet and kabar (fighting knife) for close combat. We practiced with the knives, but I was lucky not to have engaged in hand-to-hand combat. The thought of plunging the knife in someone disturbed me.

We got to know each other during the Dead Times. We'd play poker for script or just for the hell of it. We had a Recreation Tent with board games and maybe a beer. Sometimes we had Pabst beer. Most of the time we drank Asahi beer from Japan. I enjoyed the beer but wasn't much for playing games.

Some of the Marines relaxed enough to easily laugh. I was not one of those. I've never been a laid-back kind of guy. I always wanted to be, but it just wasn't and isn't me.

Scuttlebutt would circulate on the progress of the war and possible peace talks. I eventually tired of speculating when the killing would end. It raised false hopes that made duties more difficult when the Dead Times ended, as they always did.

A deadly Dead Time

I looked forward to the Dead Times because we could take a shower with a bar of Marine-issued soap. The showers were a bit crude but we could stand under a stream of water and wash away dirt and residue from our times at the front.

When in the field, we'd just dip our helmets into a pond or stream and pour the water over us to lessen the crud and dirt. At first, I didn't like using brown-colored stream water, but as time went on, I accepted it as the best alternative.

The Dead Times refreshed us for what was coming in the days to follow. I never wanted them to end, even though they did get boring.

Boring enough that one day, guys in my platoon asked me to go hunting with them. "Hunting for what?" I asked.

Deer, they told me. "It'll be fun. We'll grab some beer, have some laughs and maybe get some venison."

I thought they were nuts, but what the hell, they were buddies and I was pleased they'd invited me. It might break the dull stagnation of down time.

About eight of us wandered through the woods, following well-trodden paths, drinking beer, telling off-color jokes, and making noise. Finally, one of the corporals said we should quiet down or we'd scare the deer away.

So we walked quietly along, and sure enough, spotted a deer on a little ridge. The Marines lifted their M1's and several fired at once. The deer was a tall skinny creature, kind of like an elongated coyote. I watched as the poor animal was blown to bits by the barrage of bullets. There was nothing left to bring back.

I found the killing cruel and disgusting. We went back to drinking and partying as we followed the paths back to camp.

The next day the same guy, a corporal named Ken, came to me again. "Doc, wasn't that fun yesterday? We're goin' out again so get ready." I thanked him, but I had "stuff" to do and couldn't go. I had learned their idea of fun differed from mine.

About five hours later I heard a commotion at the battalion aid station receiving tent as they treated wounded Marines. Opening the flap, I spotted Ken on a stretcher, his head bandaged and his arm in a sling.

A deadly Dead Time

His story was frightening and sad. Seven of my platoon went hunting. Only two came back OK. Ken and two others suffered bad wounds, and the other two died. Chinese snipers had infiltrated south of the front and strapped themselves in trees waiting for patrols to attack.

The hunting party stumbled onto the wrong path. They had no chance against the snipers, well camouflaged and deadly shooters.

Orders went out that no one would leave the camp except for authorized patrols. The next day, I escorted Ken to a helicopter for transport to a ship for more treatment. A doctor said he'd survive but might lose the use of his arm.

At Marine boot camp, instructors urged us to avoid unnecessary risks and remain on alert. We felt safe when south of the front at the 38th Parallel. We were wrong.

I've not gone deer hunting again.

8

Payback
Korea, 1951

Sometimes, though, the Korean front felt like hunting. Sometimes hunting for revenge.

An urgent call had come from the 38th Parallel for relief, spurring us to hurry, grab our backpacks and weapons and assemble for departure. Orders were to relieve Marines who'd suffered a serious defeat.

We climbed off our trucks in a cold drizzle below the battered hillside. I looked up but could only see about 50 feet through the fog. The tattered Marines, who five days ago occupied the high ground, were scattered on the side of the road. At least 40 bodies waited silently in a clearing next to the road. Wounded filled stretchers ready to be evacuated. The exhausted and beat-up Marines lifted dead comrades onto the trucks for the trip to the battalion aid station.

The officers of both companies huddled for a brief time. I watched as the row of trucks carrying their sad cargo headed south. Whenever I saw death and maiming, a terrible feeling opened in the pit of my stomach. It seemed war had cheapened life, and we too readily accepted death and casualties as an everyday occurrence.

Officers decided our company didn't have the gear needed to drive the Chinese off the high ground. Instead, our platoon's lieutenant said we'd try a stealth operation. We'd infiltrate the Chinese forces at night and "give these bastards some of their own medicine."

"Our mission is to scare the shit out of 'em, killing as many as we can in their foxholes and behind their barricades."

It was payback. We'd also soften them up for the next company that would come equipped with the firepower needed to retake the high ground.

The lieutenant said, "I need 25 volunteers." About 35 of the 45 members of our platoon raised their hands. The lieutenant handpicked 25, told them what they needed to bring and to be ready at dusk. "I also need a corpsman and an alternate. Who wants to volunteer?"

The words of my Camp Pendleton drill instructor surged into my head, *Never ever volunteer for anything.* No hands went up. The lieutenant looked at his list and without expression said, "Adreon, you are our corpsman. Now, I need an alternate." A corpsman buddy of mine named Sammy raised his hand. *I knew that the alternate would join the operation only if I was killed or disabled.*

Payback

Once again, I was victim of an alphabetical list.

The darkness moved in with fog and the drizzle continued. We started up the slope in teams of four. The riflemen carried only their M1s and I carried my carbine and medkit. We needed to carry as little as possible for agility and speed.

When we approached their machine guns, we split up, sometimes zig-zagging in short spurts and sprints, mostly

crawling in silence up the slope. We kept our weapons in front, as taught back at Pendleton.

I was behind the first team when some loose rocks came dislodged and tumbled down the hillside. We feared the Chinese heard because high-pitched voices suddenly arose from the machine gun nests. We lay on the cold wet ground in full silence. After about 10 minutes, we squirmed one by one past the machine guns.

My group heard voices and followed them to a foxhole. When close enough to see it, the corporal gave a signal and we moved fast, bent low, weapons ready. They heard us coming but didn't know where to fire. They yelled as we aimed into the dark hole. We opened fire, spraying the pit with bullets.

The yelling stopped. We retreated behind a large boulder, reloaded and waited. I had fired a full clip of 30 rounds. As a corpsman, I wasn't required to approach the hole; I felt it was my duty to join in.

We heard firing from other fire teams. The Chinese had come alive. Bullets zinged and ricocheted off the boulder. The firing of a Thompson submachine gun pinned us down. Two members of our team unhooked their grenades from their web belts, pulled the cotter pin, and let them fly. The explosions caused the boulder to shake. The machine gun grew quiet.

We rolled out of our hiding place, lucky that the fog was dense and visibility almost zero. We crawled to the hill's edge and began quickly sliding down. They could hear us but still couldn't see us. They fired blindly. We saw flashes of light.

Looking up through the drizzle and smoke, we also saw explosions near the hills' top. Our guys below were helping by lobbing mortar shells at the Chinese.

We all made it back. All of us had cuts and bruises from the crawl up and slide down. Only two men had minor bullet wounds. Payback didn't come without its risks, but we'd been lucky this time.

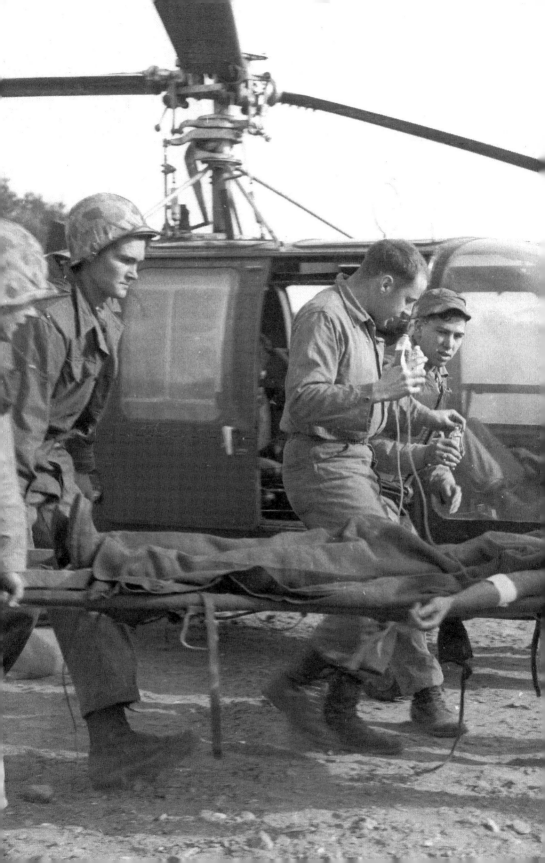

9

The bet
California, 1950

At Camp Pendleton, we were all green enough to feel lucky. I made a bet with a good friend, a guy we called Darry.

He and I joked around one day. "Let's make a bet: $100 to whoever lives the longest," Darry said. I took it and we shook. Then he laughed. "How's the winner gonna collect?"

I met Darry when I first arrived at the camp for training. He was sly, fun, feisty, and mischievous, sporting an attitude of invincibility. He wasn't a big guy, maybe five foot eight with a wiry build. But he moved as quick as a greyhound and was strong, always the first over the wall on the obstacle course.

Darry's green eyes glistened when he laughed, as he often did. His thick blond hair in the Marine Corps buzz cut looked like a wheat field after harvest.

We became buddies almost as soon as we met. We sat together in the mess hall, drank a beer in the rec area, and played ping pong, (*I was better*). He would smoke. I didn't. I'd lecture him on smoking's dangers. With a smirk, he would scoff in his friendly way.

Weekends on liberty became an adventure with Darry. We'd go to Tijuana, Mexico. The "cool" place in Tijuana was the arena for Jai-Alai, an exciting game to watch. The crowd screamed raucously for their team. The players, wearing elongated woven baskets (*xistera*), flung the ball (*pelota*) at great speed against the wall. Players tried to catch the ball before it hit the floor.

We didn't understand much about the game but liked the excitement. Gamblers gathered at the Jai-Alai Palace to place bets, meet women and drink tequila. We didn't gamble, but enjoyed the sense of lawlessness.

When our training at Pendleton ended, Darry and I crossed the Pacific on the same ship, along with 5,000 other Marines. On hot nights, we often took our sleeping bags together to the deck to get some air.

We already talked about what we'd do after the war when we returned from Korea. Darry showed me a picture of a colorful, shiny chrome-enhanced Harley that he was saving money to buy. He described the roar of the motor, the acceleration, the sustained speed, the sharp turns, even the helmet and the bike outfit he'd wear. He whetted my appetite to the thrill of a bike.

The bet

Korea, 1951

Although stationed at the same base camp, we were assigned to different companies. Most of the time, he was at the 38th Parallel when I was at the battalion aid station. When I was at the 38th, Darry was back at the base.

Once, though, I temporarily was assigned to his company. That reunited me briefly with other corpsmen I'd known at Pendleton, including Darry. I enjoyed visiting and working with him again if only for a few days. It had the flavor of a reunion.

After a few days, I returned to Dog Company. I'd rested, had a great time with Darry and others, and felt energized. Darry and the other Marines headed back to the front.

One day not long after, I helped a doctor in the receiving tent as wounded came on stretchers. Like an ER triage operation, we sorted them into categories, usually Urgent, Serious, Ambulatory or Dying. The doctor would decide where to send each Marine for treatment. After helping with initial treatment, we corpsmen arranged for the men to get to their destination for further treatment.

That day brought a steady flow of wounded. The tent flap opened and a stretcher landed in front of the doctor and me. The Marine's torn uniform was covered in mud. The right side of his face was a mass of swelling and blood. He was unconscious.

The doctor worked on him for a short time, turned to me and said, "We can't handle this here. He needs to go to the hospital ship." We got him to the copter pad in a hurry and were lucky a copter was there. Minutes later, it took off heading south.

The next day, back at the receiving tent, things were quiet. The battle at the 38th was over and we caught up on paperwork. I spotted Darry's name among those we'd treated the day before.

I asked the doctor about Darry. "Adreon, you took that Marine to the copter yesterday."

I couldn't believe it. I had watched the doctor treat him, and *I didn't recognize my best friend.*

I walked to the empty copter pad to ask when the copter was expected back. I returned, but the copter was late. I sat and waited. I had a bad feeling.

The copter descended with a roar and the pilot climbed down. Before I could ask, he said he was sorry about my fellow corpsman I'd brought to the copter. "He never made it to the ship."

The next day, I was off duty. I sat on my bunk feeling as low as I'd ever felt. I remembered the stupid bet. With my eyes closed, I saw the Harley that would never carry Darry. He was 20 years old. I wanted to scream. I wanted to cry.

I slowly walked out into the woods. Alone, I couldn't stop the tears. I reached into my holster and took out my pistol. Self pity turned into anger. I lifted the gun holding it in both hands and aimed at the sky. I shot repeatedly. A

The bet

couple of Marines came running out yelling, "What's going on?"

Pulling my cap down over my eyes so they couldn't see the tears, I turned to them and said, "Just practicing."

10

Dodging mortars
Korea, 1951

At least we brought our wounded, dying and dead back with us, whenever possible. The Chinese often didn't bother.

Digging graves for Chinese dead was one of the saddest and most horrific things on the battlefield. The stench of death was unbearable. We spoke no words, focused on the digging, and then lifted and deposited the bloated, decaying bodies into the crude, shallow trenches that would be their graves.

Sometimes, if the body had sat for days, maggots and flies feasted on the Chinese flesh. I was haunted by mothers, fathers, siblings or girlfriends in China who lost loved ones, but never would know how or where.

The digging usually came after successfully taking another hill, which always came at great cost to ourselves and the Chinese. We'd get temporarily squared away the first night at the top. The battle had ended and we'd treated our wounded, loading them on stretchers to be carried down to a forward aid station in a tent at the bottom.

Once caught up with wounded Marines, we treated the Chinese wounded and sent them down as POW's. Then, during the daylight hours, we worked to fortify our positions so we could repel a Chinese counterattack.

Foxhole duty was wearing on me. Assaulting a hill came with intense trauma, but the furious activity gave us no time to think.

In contrast, nights on the hill came with the long, eerie blackness of Korean nights and unrelenting fear of a Chinese counterattack. Tension hung amid the silence.

We didn't talk, not wanting to give away our positions to possible infiltrators. We took turns sleeping and keeping watch. Most nights, occasional mortars and exploding shells broke the silence. The Chinese blew their bugles and whistles. They were out there but we didn't know where.

Some of the guys slept so soundly that we had to jostle them with our weapons to wake them. I couldn't relax enough to sleep well in my sleeping bag. That wasn't entirely the fault of the foxhole. I've never been able to relax enough for a good sleep—the foxhole just made it more difficult. I still don't sleep soundly.

Being a corpsman brought added terror, the inevitable dreaded call from a nearby foxhole of "Corpsman! Corpsman! Hurry!"

One night I responded, slinging my carbine over my

Dodging mortars

shoulder, grabbing my med kit, tightening my helmet and preparing to move toward the calling Marine. I waited a minute or two for a lull in the mortar barrage. I then began a dash through the darkness.

I ran about 20 steps when a sudden flash temporarily blinded me, a burst of sound deafened me, and a violent explosion flung me through the air. I landed hard against a boulder on my right shoulder, neck and head. My helmet flew off. I was stunned but conscious.

I groped for my helmet and felt warm sticky blood trickling down from my face and neck. The right side of my jacket was torn and my shoulder exposed. A couple of minutes later I felt myself being dragged and pushed into a foxhole. Someone opened my med kit, grabbed some bandages and told me to hold them against the right side of my face to stop the bleeding.

"Do you need morphine?"

I said I was OK, no morphine. I stayed quiet in the foxhole for the rest of the night. I was as lucky as a Marine can get. The next morning, I made it back to my foxhole and, except for some swelling and a bunch of cuts and bruises, was not hurt. My buddies even joked that I'd tried for a Purple Heart and couldn't even do that right.

A few days later, the doctor looked me over back at the battalion station. He asked the usual questions to test if my mind was clear. I couldn't remember the name of President Truman's vice president.

No matter. I was cleared to return to my unit.

Pathway to Wars

11

Direct hit
Korea, 1951

Although I'd barely escaped a mortar hit, it was another hilltop barrage that was my worst in Korea. None was as intense. It was as if the Chinese were angry because we'd inflicted heavy casualties as we'd pushed them off the high ground.

To secure our position, we'd found or created foxholes or barricades to shield us against enemy shelling. On top of a huge, deep shell crater at the edge of the hill, seven Marines built a barricade using logs and sandbags for their protection. The barricade would guard against shrapnel from artillery or mortar shells landing nearby.

There was no protection if the Chinese got lucky and their shells found a foxhole. Mine was about 40 yards to the left. Sammy took cover in another on the other side, a similar distance away. We dug in for the night.

We'd barely finished when the furious bombardment began. I'd never seen so many shells landing. Their artillery and mortars had free rein from below, from crevices where our planes couldn't reach them.

The night filled with the cacophony of war. Vibrations shook us from the bursting shells; ear-splitting explosions were backed by the distant shrill of Chinese bugles and whistles. Sleep was impossible for the weary Marines. The ringing in my ears was all too familiar.

A sudden, blinding blast flashed over us as a shell landed close.

Luck had run out. "Direct hit, direct hit, corpsmen now!"

I leapt from my hole, raced to where I'd seen the explosive burst of light. I was the first corpsman at what was left of the nearby barricade, its logs and sandbags strewn down the hill. I took my small penlight and slid down the crater's side.

At the bottom was the most unbelievable sight. My beam of light first found a headless torso. Debris covered limbs and body parts everywhere. The direct hit had blown the Marines apart.

Sammy and two other corpsmen arrived. We looked for signs of life. Sammy signaled me to come to him, where I heard a faint moan. A large Marine's body lay on top of another. We struggled to pull him off and underneath found another with his body intact.

I checked for a pulse. Alive, miraculously. Together, Sammy and I pulled him across what seemed a river of blood mixed with dismembered remains. With the help of two other

Direct hit

corpsmen, we got the living out of the crater to check his condition.

He was unconscious. Incredibly, we could find no obvious wounds and no blood, except from the body that had covered him. We got him into another foxhole for the night. One of the corpsmen stayed with him.

Like so many others, his fate is unknown to me.

In the morning light, litter bearers brought body bags to the crater. We sent the remains of the other six Marines down the hill. We didn't know how to separate the parts into a whole so we gathered them as best we could into six separate bags. We found only four dog tags to go with the body bags.

Those Marines did everything they could to protect themselves. They didn't have a prayer.

The following night we hunkered down on the same hill, the darkness quiet as the Chinese apparently had pulled away. I tried to close my eyes but couldn't hide from the images of the night before. I still can't.

Adreon: boot camp graduate

12

Sink or swim
Missouri, 1944

The horror of Korea was unimaginable when I got drafted because, for one, it wasn't even the war that I got drafted for.

I made my first and only visit to a federal courthouse in St. Louis to answer my conscription notice in 1944. The second world war raged and that we were meeting the draft board didn't surprise anyone in the room.

We crowded the small space. Tension and uncertainty filled what air was left. We clumped in small groups, talking in whispered voices waiting for something to happen. Maybe we thought nothing would happen if nobody could hear us.

A door opened and two men walked briskly to a table. The room grew deathly quiet. One began reading a list in a harsh tone. "Adreon, Leonard J, Naval Training Center, Great Lakes, Illinois."

Why are all lists alphabetical?

No time to celebrate after my graduation from Soldan High School that year. No time either for career planning. My dad had told me there was no college in my future. "College costs money. We have no money."

Now my immediate future was pre-planned for me. Dad seemed pleased when I told him the Navy had drafted me. He'd been Navy in World War I.

Seventeen years old, just out of high school and ready, if not anxious, to begin my military career. Like so many others I had not chosen to join the military. That robbed me of the heroism of those who rushed to fight for their country. But I accepted it and embraced the draft as an adventure into the unknown.

Illinois, 1944

Boot camp at Great Lakes revealed much about me. We soon got over being strangers, sleeping in those triple-stacked barracks. We washed, showered, even went to the toilet in groups. Privacy went out the window.

That was new for most of us. I found it uncomfortable but could handle it. The loss of privacy traumatized some enough to send them to hospitals. I felt sorry for them. I don't know if they finally adjusted or the Navy dismissed them.

Each morning started with a loud screaming voice: "Drop your cocks, grab your socks, on the grinder in 20 minutes."

Sink or swim

**Postcard from Great
Lakes Naval Training Station**

Such was the crudity of boot camp. We mustered on the grinder, a large paved area next to the barracks, and followed with exercises like push ups. After calisthenics, we ran the grinder and then broke into training groups.

Boot camp lasted eight weeks or so. Indoctrination filled the first week—along with issuing uniforms and barrack assignments came lectures on protocol, rules, and restrictions. Each week had a different theme for transforming kids into sailors.

One day, officers issued us swim trunks for a swim test. Here I was in the Navy, and I couldn't swim. My mother had witnessed her younger brother drown in an Illinois lake just after his high school graduation. To protect my brother and me from the same fate, she never let us near a pool. We grew up scared of water, and without learning to swim.

I told the instructor that I didn't know how to swim. "Yeah, I hear that from a lot of you guys," the instructor said, suggesting we all just wanted into the swim classes because they sounded like more fun than other training. So we had to take the test—no big deal, jump into 12-foot deep water.

"We'll know right away if you can swim or not."

Soon, I stood on a platform above the water, pleading with the instructor. He scoffed. "Adreon, you're next. Jump!"

I stood there. "Goddamn it, jump and jump now!"

My whole body tensed. I broke into a heavy sweat. Another instructor approached me on the platform. I jumped.

My arms flailed wildly, totally out of control. Two guys came in after me. I was strong, a solid 6-foot tall at about 185 pounds. In my thrashing, I whacked one guy in the jaw. Now he needed help. Somebody rescued both of us. I went into the swimming class.

Then I flunked those classes. Maybe because at each, the instructor yelled over and over again, "Relax, you stupid bastard, relax."

Have I mentioned, I don't know how to relax?

Flunking, however, didn't disqualify me from service. I'm embarrassed. I still can't swim.

Boot camp dragged to an end. I had learned how to deal with a bunch of guys. I made friends, finding most OK and disliking a few.

Sink or swim

The military imposed its life on me. It was not my nature to live with every moment programmed. Like everyone else, I had no choice so I made the best of it. I graduated with time to visit St. Louis and celebrate with my family.

They loved my new uniform. They especially liked the cute white hat.

Adreon

13

P for Protestant
Illinois, 1944

They say there are no atheists in foxholes. I quickly learned they're not allowed on Navy ships, either.

That lesson came soon after arriving at the Great Lakes boot camp. We herded into a processing hall—my first day as a member of the herd.

I sat before a man in uniform who first wanted information for my dog tags. (I don't know what a dog has to do with this bit of metal I would hang around my neck). The early answers came easy: name, birthdate, blood type. Then, "What is your religion?"

"None," I answered without hesitation.

The interviewer looked up and said, "That is not an answer. I repeat, what is your religion?"

His simple question threw me. Growing up, my family practiced no religion. Part of my dad's family was Episcopalian,

Mom's parents were Jewish. My parents didn't worship in any way. My brother and I didn't go to Sunday school like other kids.

Meekly aggravated, I said, "I have no religion." His smirk suggested he thought I was a bad person.

"Bullshit," he said, glaring at me. "Everybody has a religion."

I thought back to playing basketball one year for the Church of the Ascension. To play, I had to belong to the church. I told Dad. "What does it cost?" he asked.

"It doesn't cost anything," I said, adding that they just passed a basket at the services.

"OK," Dad said. "As long as everyone understands that we don't pay anything."

I told the interviewer about my brief time at the Church of the Ascension. "That's good enough for me," he said, and stamped a big "P" on the form. "P" is for Protestant, he said, and so it was that I was a "P" in the Navy.

Later, I sang hymns in the Great Lakes Naval Church choir. My favorite hymn: "Onward Christian Soldiers."

Looking back, I was uncomfortable in high school not having a religion. All my friends were Catholic, Protestant, Jewish or something. My school offered no religious classes. On my own, I checked out books on religions from the local library.

I read that Catholicism, Protestantism and Judaism ranked as the big three in the United States. To me, they all seemed more alike than different. Islam, Shinto, Buddhism and other faiths also fascinated me.

P for Protestant

Finally, I made a mental list of what seemed OK religions in case I got married. Her religion would decide my religion. If we had children, they would not be like me. They would have a religion.

It all worked out. My brother became a Lutheran (first wife) then an Episcopalian (second wife). I am Jewish because my wife, Audrey, was Jewish.

Next came learning all the Navy jobs, and what I'd be trained for. We watched a film depicting all the jobs and were asked to state a preference. I was impressed we had a choice.

I chose aerographer's mate. The aerographer predicts weather conditions for pilots, which sounded scientific and exciting. I saw myself on a huge aircraft carrier somewhere on the high seas.

A few days later, orders came that I would train as a hospital corpsman. Stunned, I had no interest in medicine. I didn't like the idea of injuries, sickness and blood.

So much for having any choice in the Navy. Well, at least I'd be safe on a ship somewhere at sea and not a grunt amid the mud, chaos and death of a ground war.

Hospital corpsman third class insignia

14

The hill we lost
Korea, winter 1951

Chaos it was at the top of one hill, where my training seemed inadequate; everything seemed confusing, everyone seemed befuddled. "The Chinks are coming!" our corporal yelled. "Be ready."

Then whistles joined the bugles. And for the first time, I heard what sounded like cymbals. The Chinese had gotten close enough for us to hear them screaming and yelling in whiny, high-pitched voices. The noise made coordination impossible.

A sergeant, running from hole to hole, yelled, "Move out. We're outa here." I climbed out of the foxhole and followed my platoon down the hill. The adrenalin flowed. The Chinese had simply overwhelmed us with numbers.

It was a long way from a ship. But I'd accepted I was another grunt.

Earlier, we'd felt secure at the top. My company had arrived to relieve tired troops who had taken the hill. We expected a routine holding action. We saw it was quiet down the north side, no Chinese in sight.

Machine gunners guarded the slope with plenty of ammo. Though we'd arrived three days earlier, we still felt fresh and rested.

Looking back, maybe it was too quiet. No mortars or shells came our way. None of the usual whistles or bugles at night.

On the fourth night, Chinese artillery and mortars opened up, going after our machine gun emplacements.

We called for air support but no Corsairs responded. I don't know why.

No moon or stars shone that night. Just before dawn, we detected movement on the twisting road that came up the north slope. Mortars and artillery shells started raining down with unusual intensity, pinning us in foxholes. Then, the bugles blared.

Here they come.

Unlike the Marines, the Chinese usually attacked at night. They moved rapidly in formation up the road. Many of them carried American-made Thompson sub-machine guns captured from the Nationalists, an American ally they'd defeated in a recent civil war in China.

Our machine gunners opened up. I heard the Chinese yelling and saw flashes of light as they went after our machine guns. Exploding shells lit the area.

The hill we lost

Our gunners wreaked havoc on the Chinese but they were relentless, continuing to charge despite heavy losses. We launched flares so we could measure the enemy's strength. The flares turned the darkness into light like a fireworks display on the Fourth of July.

Then came the orders to move out. We'd never gotten that order before. But we didn't panic. We slid, rolled, ran, fell and got up, moving quickly down the hillside. Through the mist and smoke we saw shadows above us.

The Chinese wore their white quilted jackets, firing in our direction. When we could grab firm footing, we'd stop, brace ourselves and fire at the shadows. Their white was to blend in with winter snow, but it made them stand out in the semi-darkness. Our sharpshooters with their scoped rifles inflicted massive casualties.

The Chinese followed us down the hill just a bit. They shouted, screamed and fired at us until we'd escaped their range. Like us before, they were content to take the hill and hold it.

Although they still fired mortars, most of the damage was done. Our company re-grouped and I worked the hillside to treat the wounded.

Stretcher bearers removed the wounded and then began the grim task of removing those who had died. The Marines, unlike the Chinese, tried hard to leave no one behind.

At the bottom, we set up tents along the main road and battened down. Officers decided we were in no condition to retake the hill. We would wait for relief.

The retreat exhausted us. Individually, none of us could understand what was happening beyond our immediate area. All we could do was to wait for orders, try to keep the adrenaline under control, and execute the orders as best we could.

Confusion always heightened the terror.

Adreon's ambulance at Northwestern University

15

Final duty WWII
Illinois, 1945

Back in World War II, I had missed fighting altogether. My initial adventure, in fact, finished at a first-class private university.

A train from the corpsman school in Idaho had pulled into Chicago, Ill. I transferred alone with my duffel to another train for Evanston, just north of the city.

A college town on the shores of Lake Michigan, Evanston struck me as odd combination of old-line conservative families aside the less-inhibited students at Northwestern University.

Well Dad, I finally made it to college, though not as a student. I reported to the sick bay on the second floor of Patten Gymnasium on Sheridan Road, which also housed the Navy sleeping quarters.

What could be better for a basketball enthusiast than to live above a gym?

My boss was Chief Petty Officer Jeff from Joplin, Mo., a high school basketball coach in Joplin before getting called back to service. He was much older, maybe 35 or 40.

By the way, I find it curious that the word petty means *of little importance or trivial.* I was a third class petty officer (HM3) meaning that I was much less important than a chief petty officer. *I still think the Navy can find a better tag for these positions.*

For the most part I enjoyed my world war duty. We treated sailors when sick or injured. It was not challenging.

But there was the one cold night I was called back from our sleeping quarters because of a seriously ill sailor. The doctor treated him for some sort of respiratory problem. "Adreon, we need to get him to the hospital at Great Lakes."

We bundled him up and brought him to the entrance where I'd parked our only ambulance. It was some sort of stretch vehicle, pretty beat up from a previous accident.

With the patient strapped to a stretcher in the back, I drove the Skokie Highway heading north. Heavy skies soon opened up, dumping buckets of snow. I could hardly see the pavement.

I was not an experienced driver. In fact, I learned to drive mostly by driving the ambulance at that base. I certainly had never driven in blizzard conditions.

Add to that, I wasn't sure I could find the hospital, while the guy in back struggled with his breathing. I spotted and followed a large, over-the-road truck.

Final duty WWII

I had no way to check the sailor in the back. My shoulders grew tight, my hands and knuckles white from gripping the wheel.

The truck turned off the highway. I slowed, squinting through the snow as his lights shone on a sign: *GREAT LAKES NAVAL TRAINING CENTER.*

Relieved, I followed the truck into the base. The guard at the entrance gave me directions to the hospital. I pulled up to the emergency entrance, where my patient was taken into the ER.

A blessed nurse came out to say the sailor would be OK. Too exhausted to drive back, I asked where I could spend the night. She offered an empty room where I fell into the bed, glad that ordeal was over.

Most of the rest of my time at Northwestern was a lot less stressful, even fun. I often traveled with the football team because several Navy guys played, and well, regulations required that a corpsman and a Navy doctor accompany them.

We played at Indiana to a 7/7 tie. We lost to Ohio State by a couple of points. Notre Dame clobbered us late in the season. The atmosphere of big-time college football thrilled me: roaring crowds, marching bands, *GO YOU NORTHWESTERN,* the color and the cheerleaders. All exciting.

One of the Navy players on our team was Max Morris, who played end and made All American in 1944. He also led the basketball team. The basketball coach let me work out with the team during practice sessions at the Patten gym. The team tolerated me, though I was younger.

I enjoyed the college experience, even if I wasn't a student. Attractive coeds made us feel welcome and comfortable. I attended bonfires and other gatherings. We went to Cooley's Cupboard, popular with the co-ed crowd for their curlicue French fries.

Home to the Women's Christian Temperance Union (WCTU), Evanston barred liquor. So the sophisticated crowd went across the Chicago border to beer joints on Howard Street. Even I went a few times for the experience. I grew to like the frosted mugs of draft beer, and enjoyed the flirting and sometimes-raucous times.

My chief made fun of my inexperience, but we developed a friendship that continued for a while after the war. He called me *Junior*. I once visited Chief Jeff in Joplin. I later worked as an usher at Sportsman Park, where the Cardinals and the Browns played, and got tickets to a few Cardinal baseball games for him and his Joplin friends.

Jeff later faded from my life, like so many of the military faces I'd known.

I clearly remember the death of President Roosevelt in the spring of 1945. Less than a month later, the war in Europe ended and the nation celebrated VE day. The war itself ended in September, after the atomic devastation of Hiroshima and Nagasaki, and the Japanese signed a surrender on the battleship Missouri.

Final duty WWII

The Navy released me shortly afterward. But they said, hey, I could join the U.S. Naval Reserve. I'd get paid if I attended reserve meetings.

Having grown up in the Great Depression, my impulse was to never turn down a buck. I signed up. Besides, the war had just ended so the Navy wouldn't need guys like me anymore.

I was wrong.

Happy Ending.

16

We paid too much
Korea, 1951

I had plenty of time in Korea to think how wrong I'd been. When I wasn't caught in the terror of hill warfare, that is. Two giant armies pulling and pushing to hold a hill, lose it and win it again.

The hills of Korea are not the Alps or the Rocky Mountains, but when I stood at the bottom and looked up, one hill loomed like a mountain. It was the highest in the area. We'd held it. They'd driven us off. We wanted it back.

It was cold, a colorless sky, and wet. It wasn't rain. It wasn't sleet. It wasn't snow. Icy pellets fell from the heavy grey. I stood at the foot of the mountain and gazed thousands of feet to the top. The pellets stung as they pummeled my face. I lowered my helmet.

I couldn't see the top through the mist and fog but knew the Chinese held it. We wanted it back because of how it commanded the area. From the top, the Chinese could pin us down and attack our convoys on the road below. Our command had decided this was the day to take it back.

They thought the poor visibility would hide us from the Chinese as we assembled. But the weather also meant our Corsair planes couldn't fly. We'd have no air support.

The men of my Dog Company waited in the dark. We'd added equipment because we knew it would be tough. We readied more bazookas than usual and packed lots of ammo and grenades. We'd have to take out the machine gun nests that guarded the summit.

I was one of ten corpsmen, and held my carbine loaded and ready. All of us carried an extra med pack with plenty of morphine, bandages, and iodine tubes for the wounded.

The order came as first light trickled through the clouds. We started up the hill.

At first it was quiet and the climb wasn't bad. We dodged loose rocks as they tumbled down but the slope wasn't steep.

All hell broke loose about a third of the way up.

The Chinese started firing. Visibility worsened amid exploding shells and the barrage of gunfire. We would run, hit the ground, fire at flashes of light up ahead, run and crawl as our fire teams moved in coordinated stages.

"Corpsman!" was yelled to my right and about 30 yards above. I put my head down and followed the yell. A Marine lay face down in the muck, not moving. A corporal and I turned him over but the fixed stare told us it was too late. He was our lead lieutenant.

We paid too much

The corporal removed his belt and handed it to me with the holster and a .45-caliber pistol. He said, "Take this, you might need it."

I was surprised, but before I could say anything, he'd moved on. I strapped the belt around my waist.

The next time I was back at the base, I took the .45 to the supply tent and requested ammo. The lieutenant's belt came with two packets of magazines. The gun felt heavy at more than three pounds.

Because of my medkits, I didn't have room for added pouches on my web belt. I asked the supply guy what to do, and he issued me a bandolier to wear over my shoulder to carry the .45 ammo. He also showed me how to release the safety so I could practice firing.

I took the gun out into the woods, released the safety, cocked it, held it in my right hand, my arm stiffly extended, aimed at a dead tree and pulled the trigger. My shoulder felt like it left my body from the recoil. I learned the hard way that you hold this weapon in two hands if you want to continue using your shoulder.

Even today I have limited use of my right arm. The Navy didn't give a Purple Heart for this kind of injury. The only award I deserved was a ribbon for stupidity.

Back on the giant hill, Dog Company spent hours making its way up. Slowly and tediously, we ran, crawled, and slithered through mud.

Our forces finally got far enough to attack their machine guns. We used bazookas, Browning automatics, flamethrowers and grenades to stifle the rapid firing that had taken a toll on our men.

Although it wasn't my job, I helped throw grenades at machine gun barricades. I felt compelled to do more than just treat the wounded. I repeatedly fired my carbine but couldn't measure my contribution to our assault.

The flamethrowers finished the job, spewing their mixture of oil and gas into a fierce red-yellow flame. Again came the sight of a Chinese machine gunner running out of a barricade on fire, his face blackened by the flames.

Watching him fall, his body shaking, was a brutal image of this war. Somehow, I felt better each time the shaking stopped. I knew that for him the war was over.

It took about eight hours to get to the top. The Chinese had left their positions and scurried down the north slope. We didn't follow, sticking to our assignment to secure the hill.

My fellow corpsmen and I could barely keep up with the wounded. We worked to the point of total exhaustion, even as night descended.

A parade of stretchers struggled down the hillside as corpsmen and Marines tried to control bleeding and ease pain. The Chinese had left many dead, which we stacked on the hill's north side.

We also treated the wounded that the Chinese left behind, after we'd had cared for our own. Stretcher bearers took the Chinese, now POWs, down to the base of the hill.

Two hundred and ten started up the hill, 87 reached the top.

We owned the hill.

We paid too much.

17

My college years
Missouri, 1946

After my experience at Northwestern University at the end of World War II, college beckoned again. Federal financing by way of the GI bill allowed me to study at Washington University in my hometown of St. Louis.

Dad had told me often we had no money for college, so I looked at WashU as a big bonus and became a serious student. Other veterans felt the same way. We saw a chance to prepare for a competitive world.

The ROTC program came knocking, the Reserve Officer Training Program that would enable me to become an Army officer. I turned it down. I was done with the military, though I vaguely remembered I'd signed for the Naval Reserve. My brother, Mert, later opted for the ROTC and ended up an Army Reserve colonel.

The Navy Reserve sent notices for meetings and other activities. I had no interest even though I could earn some bucks. Now that I had the GI Bill, I didn't need the Reserve.

For recreation, I played basketball. I had played in high school long ago. I started playing on an intramural team, then tried out for the WashU varsity. I made the junior varsity and worked on my game.

An assistant coach, Stan, held pedigree as a talented athlete from Springfield, Illinois. He and I'd served together briefly at Great Lakes where we became friends, sharing weekend liberty.

We also joined a YMCA basketball team in Waukegan, Illinois and played in a weekend league. Stan was great. I was better than OK. Our team was the league's best.

One memorable weekend, a team of black players came to play. It was a revelation. We played hard. They played harder. We jumped for rebounds. They jumped higher. We drove for layups. They grabbed the ball, sailed through the air and dunked baskets. They destroyed us. Stan and I sat in the stands after the game. He looked at me and nodded, "LJ," (what my teammates called me), "we just saw and experienced the future of basketball." How prophetic.

Stan worked to get me a shot at the WashU varsity team. It was a good team. Bob Light was our center, Charlie Cane a forward, the Pearce twins guards. Richard Pearce attended business school with me. His brother, David, studied architecture and planned to join his dad's firm.

My college years

I spent more time on the bench than on the court, watching our coach pace the sideline, pulling his ears as tension grew, his face a flaming red. I loved being on the team, cherished my time on the court. I proudly wore my letter sweater on and off campus.

My playing time grew during my senior year. I think we were good, though I can't remember if we won more games than we lost.

I wasn't good with the girls on campus. I blamed it on not smoking cigarettes like the popular guys. So I decided to smoke a pipe, buying aromatic tobacco sure to attract the girls. It smelled good; I thought I looked suave and cool.

Probably smoked for about a semester, particularly when girls were around. They didn't seem to notice, not a bit. The pipe burned my tongue. I gave it up.

Sportsman's Park, St. Louis, 1946

My four years went fast, split between classwork, homework, basketball and a job as an usher captain at Sportsman's Park. I was more popular on campus in 1946 when I recruited other students as ushers for the World Series. The Cards beat the Red Sox in seven games.

In my junior year, I met a bright, charming, exceptionally attractive girl named Sylvia. We dated, hung out at Yacovelli's Bar and Restaurant, went to movies and sometimes dancing.

I think Sylvia liked me. I liked her. After her junior year, her family moved. Sylvia transferred to a school in Pennsylvania. One day together, the next day she was gone. I hope she has had a good life.

I graduated in June, 1950. Dad, Mom and Grandma, my mother's mom, came to the service on the quadrangle. I remember Dad had trouble walking. He was short of breath and had to stop often. Dad died in 1952 at age 58, the year I returned from Korea.

The commencement speaker was Bernard Baruch, a prominent investor and philanthropist who I'm sure was a thoughtful guy. I don't remember what he said.

Though my family didn't have a formal celebration, I took pride in my college achievement. My good grades got me elected to Beta Gamma Sigma, the national honor society for business schools.

After graduation, I started to work for my grandfather in the insurance business.

My college years

By that time, I'd mostly forgotten about the Naval Reserve. I'd never attended a meeting and even quit opening the letters.

I was a college graduate, 24 years old, and ready to launch my civilian career.

18

Big Mike remembers Iwo Jima

Korea, summer 1951

It was on a relatively pleasant June day when our platoon gathered for mail call. We sat in a large circle outside our tent. The Marine with the bag of mail stood in the middle, opened the bag, read the envelopes and started calling out names.

I had a good day, got two pieces of mail. A short letter from my mom that somewhat irritated me as she continued to mention college graduates who were recruited into the navy and sent to Officer Candidate School in Newport, Rhode Island. This, of course, reminded me that I had applied to the same school when I was recalled but didn't get orders to go. The other letter was from my brother who was attending Washington University. He told me he had joined the ROTC and planned on active duty as an army lieutenant. My dad rarely wrote letters. Sometimes Mom's letter said that Dad sends his best.

I watched as Big Mike's name was called, saw him come forward and take his letter. Watched him rip it open and read. I noticed a deep frown and sad expression on his face. With letter in hand, he went into the tent. I knew something was wrong.

I found him sitting on his bunk holding his head in his hands. I asked, "Mike, bad news?"

He looked up. "Yeah, my best buddy on Iwo was killed in a motorcycle accident." He rubbed his eyes. "My friend, Sean, had barely survived the Jap's attacks on Iwo. We celebrated together. Sean told me he'd had enough and planned to go into civilian life as soon as he could. Tried to talk me out of staying in."

Mike shook his head and smiled a little sad smile. "Now Sean is gone and I'm still OK."

I tried to change the subject. I asked, "How tough was it on Iwo?"

"Lost a hell of a lot of men landing on that island. Japs were dug in caves and tunnels." He described how they were also in bunkers and killed a lot of Marines by firing down on the beach. The beach was covered with a kinda soft ash making it hard to move.

"We were target practice for the Japs. What finally won for us was our air power and our bombardment from the navy ships. It was ugly and bloody."

Mike paused and shook his head, "A shell burst near Sean, hot pieces of shrapnel slashed into his neck and shoulders. He was treated and sent back to the states."

Big Mike remembers Iwo Jima

Mike continued, "After our artillery shells pummeled the Japs, we cleaned out their bunkers with flame throwers, bazookas, and grenades. We were able to get into their tunnels and kill or capture them."

He squinted and said in a strong voice, "Think that this war, taking a hill, losing a hill, taking it again and again, goin' on forever is worse. At least on Iwo we kept at it until we controlled the island. Here we hunker down on a hilltop and wait for the next attack. Losing too many men in this sort of going-no-place war."

Mike scoffed, "In Iwo Jima, most of the fighting was over in less than two months. Here, I've been doin' this for many months with no end in sight."

He stood, turned and said, "I hated the killing. The Japs, even beaten, did not want to surrender. The killing continued after the island was secure. Some of 'em hid in the tunnels. We could never feel totally secure."

I was surprised that he talked so much, not his usual way. I asked, "Why did you reenlist?"

He replied, "Cause I was stupid. Thought bein' a decorated Marine in peacetime would be good duty. Didn't dream that another war could start within five years and I'd be back in all this shit."

I could see he was getting more upset. "Mike, let's go to the rec tent and get a beer, OK?"

He smiled, "Yeah, good idea."

That was the last conversation I was to have with Big Mike. His war and Marine Corps duty ended on an ugly hill later that summer.

19

My worst moment
Korea, 1951

We were in a hot, muggy summer stretch a little north of the 38th Parallel when my Dog Company assembled at the bottom of a hill. It was dark. The hill was quiet. Mosquitoes attacked. I wondered if our repellent repelled or attracted. I hated the insidious buzz in my ear.

Our lieutenant signaled for us to gather. "We've got orders," he said. "We're goin' up this hill. Chinks are dug in, so it'll be tough. Bring plenty of ammo."

"You, corpsman," pointing at me, "Be sure your medkits are full. We move out at first light."

It was a dark night. No moon, no stars, heavy clouds, a mist in the air. I checked my carbine, my .45 pistol, and refilled my medkits. I was ready. The lieutenant ordered, "Move out."

Big Mike led our squad. A powerfully-built Marine, he projected a rough, tough-guy manner that hid a kind heart. We knew he had our backs.

Everyone in our platoon had been touched by Mike's horrendous combat stories from Iwo Jima in World War II, and on the miserable hillsides of Korea.

Whatever we had learned and forgotten in Marine boot camp, Big Mike made sure we kept our heads down, crawled with our weapons in front and kept ourselves in condition. We felt fortunate to have him in our company.

The mist turned to rain, not unusual in those hills even in the dead of summer. The slope proved difficult. Water cascaded down. The slimy ground made it tough to get traction. I thought, a bad day for a climbing assault.

About 90 minutes into the climb, we heard the Chinese bugles sounding attack. I was surprised they could see us through the foggy rain. They lobbed mortar shells, followed by artillery shelling. We wanted Marine Corsairs to attack. Visibility made that impossible.

The Chinese swarmed in large numbers down the hill towards us, firing rifles, burp guns and launching grenades. It became obvious they outnumbered our forces. As we had learned in earlier battles, they came regardless of their losses. There was something suicidal about their attack.

Suddenly, a grenade landed to my left. Big Mike saw it, grabbed it and threw it into a gully. The grenade exploded, a fiery blast. I felt the vibration. He had saved his lead fire team.

My worst moment

Two or three hours into the fight, we had made progress but the Chinese kept coming. Mike was still in the lead position, a guy with a Browning automatic at his side. They fired their weapons, clearing a way for the rest of us.

His BAR guy was hit and went down. Mike rushed over. I heard the staccato firing from a burp gun. Now Mike was hit. His helmet flew off. His arms flew up. He grabbed his neck, falling forward, rolling and shaking on the wet ground. I was there in seconds. Blood spurted from his neck. I pulled bandages from my medkit and pressed hard on his neck.

I couldn't stop the bleeding. Mike's mouth was open. He tried to speak. Nothing. Red, sticky blood covered his body. He had no chance. The bleeding stopped. His eyes glazed over. He was gone.

Within minutes, the order came to fall back. Our machine gunners and flame throwers positioned themselves to stop the Chinese from chasing us. The rest of us slipped and slid down the hill. Stretcher bearers collected the wounded as we moved down the hill. The choking smell of cordite and garlic filled the air as the Chinese kept coming.

Finally, they stopped their reckless pursuit. Our gunners had extracted a heavy toll. The firing quieted. Ilooked back and saw the enemy standing on the hillside watching our retreat. Then, they pulled toward the hilltop. We continued down.

Our stretcher bearers went to find and retrieve dead Marines. I couldn't bear the thought that Big Mike lay somewhere up there. I climbed back to him.

He was lying on his back, his unseeing eyes staring at the sky. I touched his face, wiped away the clotted black blood, gently closed his eyes and yelled for a stretcher.

The stretcher came and I asked to help carry him down, the first and only time I helped evacuate a fallen Marine. Mike was heavy. I struggled to hold my end over the tough terrain.

I helped load Big Mike onto the truck that would carry him and other Marines back to the base. The start of a long, sad journey home.

I spied a huge boulder, sat behind it, took off my helmet, put down my carbine and, holding my head in my hands, burst into tears. I didn't care if anyone saw. If anyone did, not a word was said.

It was my worst moment in Korea, and I sensed I wouldn't be the same. I struggled to grasp the feelings—a deeply disturbing mix of sick, angry, disgusted and above all, sad.

Big Mike's quick instincts and bravery enable me to write this. He was one of many quiet, unheralded heroes damaged or destroyed in war. I owe him so much. We owe them so much.

Sailor, Civilian, Marine

The recall meant Adreon would soon be a Marine (above).

20

The recall
Illinois, 1950

The letter arrived with a thud. They'd changed my Naval Reserve status from "inactive" to "active."

War had broken out in a faraway place, Korea. OK, career interrupted—but not life threatening. I'd serve on a ship, and if I'd thought about it, North Korea probably didn't even have a Navy.

I'd been feeling like hot stuff before that letter arrived: a Bachelor of Science in Business Administration, top 5% of my class at Washington University.

A fantastic career awaited. My grandfather, an insurance broker with the Charles L. Crane agency, had invited me to join him at the agency. I immediately went to work, spending two months learning the casualty business, including a trip to Philadelphia for a special course. I readied to go forth and sell insurance to the world.

Instead, the Navy told me I was to report in 30 days to the Navy base at Great Lakes, Illinois. My mistake back in 1945 had resurfaced. Now I made a second trip to the Great Lakes base.

With college diploma in hand and my scholastic honors, I quickly told the Navy I wanted to become an officer. I filled out the forms and interviewed with three officers, who impressed me with their thoroughness. They explained I needed to show the maturity to be an officer. I thought I had.

An intense physical followed, and I passed. The officers told me that when selected, not if, I would head to Newport, Rhode Island for 90 days of officer training. Their report and all the information would go to the Navy's personnel bureau in Washington D. C.

I imagined myself in a sharp-looking Navy officer outfit.

Meanwhile, they assigned me to the hospital at the base. Marines from Korea filled most of the beds, with the battered and wounded men telling their sad and often tragic stories. I treated seriously wounded for the first time. I learned to change dressings, give penicillin shots, take blood for lab testing and work with doctors.

Still stateside meant the fun didn't stop. The coach of the Great Lakes basketball team discovered I was a college player and asked me to try out. I became the starting guard. We played nearby college teams in Illinois and Wisconsin.

Twice I received orders for sea duty, once for the hospital ship with the unusual name, Repose, and once for a destroyer. Both times the coach had the orders cancelled so he wouldn't

The recall

lose his best-scoring guard. In fact, the first order came right after my finest game. I scored 28 points against DePaul University in an overtime win.

Then the coach shipped out. Shortly after, orders came for me to transfer to the fleet Marine force and report for pre-Korean training.

I'd forgotten the Navy provided medical services for the Marine Corps, the ground fighting force for the Navy. Even if I'd remembered, I would've welcomed the coach keeping me around until my orders arrived from officer-training school.

Clearly, a lofty college degree had not made this 24-year-old a smart decision maker. I'd missed being a corpsman on a destroyer or on a hospital ship, safely off the coast of Korea.

And the officer school hadn't come calling. I was about to become a Marine.

Adreon

21

From swabby to Marine
California, 1951

Duty with the Marines meant yet-another boot camp. This one at Camp Pendleton near Oceanside, Calif. In a matter of weeks, drill instructors would transform me from a civilian or Navy guy to an attacking Marine.

Despite the image the name evokes, Oceanside was no resort on a sandy beach, sipping Mai Tais while soaking up warm sun as tranquil waves splashed along the shore. My weeks there would be hectic and, in many ways, amazing.

I landed at a section of Pendleton called Camp Del Mar, located right on the Pacific Ocean. Three-tiered bunks arranged with Marine precision filled the wooden, two-story barracks that held about 30 guys per floor.

The morning after my arrival, we new arrivals got outfitted for the Marines. I remembered pictures of Marines in beautiful dress outfits and thought I'd have a similar photo for all at home to admire. Nope.

The camp issued corpsmen battlefield-drab, green-fatigue clothes for everyday wear. Only the small caduceus on one sleeve marked me as a corpsman. The caduceus is that medical symbol that looks like two serpents twisted around a winged staff.

Appearing like all the other Marines, I joined others in the first of many tents to come. A drill sergeant limped in leaning on a crude cane. He was a scruffy-looking guy, maybe 5-feet-10-inches tall, dark buzz-cut hair and a face that needed a razor. He smiled and welcomed the group.

That might've been the only smile we got from him.

"My name is Fred, you will call me *Sergeant*," he said, explaining we were there to learn about combat in Korea. He was a gunnery sergeant who'd been there and back.

He said he was lucky, coming back with shrapnel in one leg, better than what happened to a lot of his buddies. "I'm gonna make you swabbies into Marines," he said, adding that it wouldn't be easy in the little time we had. "If I succeed, you will *not* like me, but in the end, you'll thank me."

He paused and sized up the group of about 20 of us. He began with weapons, explaining that corpsmen carried carbines, asking how many had fired a rifle. No hands went up.

"They're not much good but it's all we have," he said. "I can hardly hit a target with that fuckin' gun, so just hold the trigger down and fire away."

From swabby to marine

We wouldn't leave as sharpshooters, he said, but we'd be the best we could with our weapon.

He was right. I rarely hit where I was aiming but with a full clip of 30 shells, I could rapidly fire many rounds. That gave me a sense of security.

The sergeant said we'd also learn how to use weapons meant for close combat—a bayonet and the Ka-bar, a 12-inch knife with a seven-inch, non-folding blade.

We learned how to *zero in* our weapons and take the weapon apart and put it back together in the dark.

The Marines issued us canvas backpacks that I think were called haversacks. They came in two parts. The upper, marching pack contained rations, poncho and clothes. The lower knapsack held extra shoes and maybe a change of underwear and socks. Grommet tabs on the exterior held a bayonet, shovel, a bedroll of sleeping bag and blankets, a canteen and a first aid pouch.

The heavy haversacks strained our backs—someone said they weighed 90 pounds, though I never weighed mine. We could leave part of it behind to lighten the load in combat.

One brutal exercise had us carrying the packs up a dried, sandy creek bed under a blazing sun. Some of the guys couldn't make it to the top. I struggled and wanted to lie down but made it. At 24, I was several years older than most. My basketball conditioning helped me.

We learned to keep our heads down while crawling with our weapon in front. The Marines had an effective teaching method: A machine gun fired live ammo about three feet above the ground. We crawled beneath the barrage. Later, in Korea, I appreciated what they'd taught us.

A misanthropic devil must have designed an obstacle course we ran, the toughest part of training. We crawled through narrow spaces, ran to a wall to climb over, dangling from ropes without falling into a muddy pit below and much more.

Our drill sergeant screamed and yelled every obscenity in the book, pushing us to move faster and faster. Each failure brought a torrent of you shithead, chicken, queer or worse.

From swabby to marine

They took us to sea to practice an amphibious landing. We'd climb over the side of the ship wearing a full backpack and down the cargo net that swayed from the side of the ship. A Higgins landing craft waited below to carry us to the beach.

Not knowing how to swim, I held on desperately each time. I was sure my life was over if I let go. It scared the hell out of me.

We were taught to stay alert and "at the ready." Once, sitting in class, the door burst open and two men in

Chinese-like fatigues came in firing automatic weapons. The sergeant yelled, "Get down!" and we dove under the desks. Point made.

A captain explained the Marine Corps structure, that we had become part of the First Marine Division. We'd be assigned to a regiment also designated by a number. A regiment, usually commanded by a colonel, consisted of three battalions made up of three companies, each commanded by a captain like him. A company is split into three platoons, each led by a lieutenant.

He smiled. "I see some of you taking notes. Throw them away. You don't have to remember any of that. We Marines keep it simple, we deal in groups of three."

We'd be part of a platoon made up of three squads of three, four-man fireteams. So a squad is about 13 men and a platoon about 46, allowing for two corpsmen, a radioman and a few other specialists tagging along. Numbers would designate all the groupings except for companies, which are assigned letters, like A(Able), B(Baker), C(Charlie), D(Dog), E(Easy) and F(Fox).

All we needed to know was our company and platoon, he said. The captain was right—I found out that on a day to day basis that was all I needed to know.

Not all of us finished the training. Three of the 20 couldn't cope with the strain and were reassigned, and another broke a leg on a hill climb. For the rest of us, the weeks went by too fast. It meant it was time to board a ship to cross the Pacific.

From swabby to marine

Sergeant Fred, after weeks of cursing and pushing, sent us off with two words: "Good luck."

My sailor days had ended. I was a Marine.

Semper Fi.

Semper Fidelis, latin for "Always Faithful," the Marine Corps motto.

22

Steady hands
Korea, 1951

We put some of our greatest faith in the specialists who helped keep us alive. There were the engineers, for example, who cleared our path of mines.

Highly trained, they worked in an impressive, structured manner, patiently scouring every inch of a road. They repeatedly found mines paired with booby traps. As our platoon stood back, the engineers would calmly eliminate the traps and disarm the mines.

I got to watch closely when orders came to accompany the engineers. It was a cold evening. Our platoon, then about 45 men, had gathered around a potbelly stove in the dim light of a Coleman lantern in one of the pyramidal tents at the battalion base.

Our lieutenant called us together on short notice. We'd come back recently from the front line at the 38th Parallel.

He stood tall in front of us and said, "I know we've only been back a few days, but we have orders to accompany men from the First Marine Engineering Battalion on a combat patrol."

They'd need everyone including the two corpsmen, Sam and I.

The following morning we were ready by the appointed hour of 0700. Sam and I checked our medkits, ensuring they had plenty of olive-drab combat bandages, pieces of rubber for tourniquets, morphine syrettes and the rest. I had two 30-round magazines for my M1 carbine, hand grenades, and a full bandolier of bullets for my .45 pistol.

The lieutenant explained we'd follow the engineers who'd probe for mines or booby traps set by the Chinese. Our patrol would take us along a pitted, but usable, narrow road to a village. This would be a new experience for our platoon. As usual, nobody told us why that road or that village.

We gathered at sunrise with about a dozen engineers and followed them to the road. Their job was gut wrenching—every step fraught with danger. They used metal detectors and other devices to probe the surface. They looked for well-camouflaged mines, usually in clusters of three or four, often booby trapped by grenades placed in small holes with earth packed around them.

The grenade handle was up and the cotter pin pulled with a small rock on top of the safety lever to hold it in place. A small movement could detonate the grenade. Those Marines had the hard, lean, cold-eyed look of men trying to prevent a sudden death-delivering explosion.

Steady hands

My throat grew parched, my heart pounding as I watched them with steady hands uncover and deactivate a mine. It looked like a carton of tar paper sandwiched between wood and presumably contained TNT. It was about 10 inches long and five inches wide, maybe three inches high.

I held my breath every time they found one. Amazingly, the only explosions came from booby trap grenades exploding after being removed from their hiding place and tossed aside.

Our patrol ended at a small village, my first such visit. It looked like a group of small adobe huts with thatched roofs. The engineers went inside each hut. I was told that they were looking for a place where the Chinese stored weapons, shells, or other ammunition. Our platoon helped in the search. We found nothing in the huts.

We did our best not to frighten the people of the village. They looked at us as the "good guys." There were some older

men and women in the huts and on the road. I didn't see any young people or children.

Men squatted in front of their hut, smiled and waved as we left their village. They had survived the North Korean invasion. Many had survived the brutal Japanese occupation during World War II. What a tough, sad life.

Months later, on my way home from Korea, I bought two small, hand-carved statues of an older couple that reminded me of that village. I sent them home to my parents. I see them in my den every day.

We'd return to base on the same road, stress-free knowing the mines were gone. About half way back, shots rang out. "Hit the deck!"

Two of our men went down. Sammy went to one, I rushed to the other.

Adreon's memento calls to mind the kind Korean villagers.

My Marine was an engineer. A bullet had hit him in the back near his shoulder and another bullet had grazed his neck. I controlled the bleeding with compression bandages and gave him a shot of morphine. He was conscious. His vital signs looked good. Four of our platoon placed him on a stretcher to rush him back to base.

Steady hands

While working on him, I heard loud shots from rifles and a Browning automatic. Our platoon had found the Chinese who'd attacked us. The shattering noise continued for about 15 minutes.

Then it quickly grew quiet. When I looked up, the Marines dragged the dead bodies of three Chinese snipers who had hidden in foliage at the road's edge. We were lucky to suffer only two casualties.

Safely back at base, I thought about the Marine engineers whose thankless, dangerous work reduced casualties in the roads and fields.

I was happy we weren't called to help them again.

USS General M.C. Meigs (U.S. Navy)

23

My Pacific cruise
California, 1951

So I did get on a Navy ship. As a passenger. Standing on the dock on a perfect sun-filled spring day in San Diego, I stood in awe of the massive ship sitting quietly waiting for us.

More than 600 feet long, the ship stood at least 5 stories tall with two massive smokestacks. At the age of 24, I had not anticipated I'd so quickly get an all-expense-paid Pacific cruise.

Near the anchor on the bow, written in black against the ship's drab color, was "USS General M.C. Meigs." Two lone stripes decorated the top of the smokestacks.

Two gangplanks came down. I stood with 5,200 others waiting to board. We carried our own luggage. We all looked somewhat alike.

We headed down narrow stairs into the bowels of the ship. It was quite a sight, row after row of six-high bunk beds. I don't know how anyone managed to climb to the top ones.

The officers had quarters with their own toilets and showers. Our toilets were lined up in a large room next to another room with side-by-side wash stands. I'd guess that several hundred could use those rooms at one time.

Despite the indignities of boot camp, this seemed particularly crude. Little did I know these would seem luxurious compared to the facilities that awaited us at our destination.

My first shower on ship was startling. It came in another huge space with shower heads staring down at hundreds of naked bodies. The liquid they spewed felt like mineral oil, not water.

Our bars of soap produced no lather. They simply slid across skin, giving the impression of washing off sweat and grime. We'd remember each shower because of the itching that followed. Salt water showers were like that.

The officers reportedly had fresh water. Even today, I relish my walk-in shower with a sudsy bar of Irish Spring soap, stepping out ready for another wonderful day.

Five days out of San Diego came my first storm at sea. The big, ugly ship tossed to the left, then to the right, up and down, rhythmically. Those who didn't get sick from the motion got sick from the suffering around them. The storm lasted two days.

My Pacific cruise

Trained to fight, we fought for a place on deck with its fresh air. It was quite a sight—thousands of sleeping bags within inches of each other. Except during rough weather, it became a nightly event.

At 24, I was elderly compared to most of the Marines. They were 19, 20 and 21 years of age. I didn't share their excited anticipation of arriving in a war zone. Maybe I was more mature. Maybe I was more scared.

Kim's gift to L.J.

24

A gift unexpected
Korea, 1951

It was on board the Meigs that I heard men referring to our enemy as "gooks."

By the time I got to Korea, the Chinese had entered the war on the side of the North. I'm not sure I saw any North Koreans in battle. I guess the term gooks was meant to cover the Chinese and the North Koreans. It was a term denigrating our enemy. Oddly, the difference between the North Korean gooks and the South Koreans for whom we were fighting was based on the geography of where they lived relative to the 38th Parallel.

That situation made me uncomfortable. The Koreans I met, South Koreans, were mostly cordial, even warm. My favorite was a friend and helper to the First Marine Division.

Kim Sung Hahn hung around the battalion base, and smiled from when I first saw him to when we said goodbye many months later.

When we readied to head to the front, Kim would help us gather boxes of dressings and five-gallon water cans. He also brought bundles of triage sleeping bags, which had multiple zippers for quick access to a Marine's multiple wounds.

Other old Korean men also worked at the base. Using A frames, they helped carry water, ammo, rations, stretchers and other supplies. They also endured the task of clearing ground holes we used as toilets. We called them "honey dippers." I felt sorry for the men with the withered faces doing those ugly jobs. The Korean army had taken away most of the younger men.

Kim was a quiet kind man, probably more than 60 years old, skinny and bent over, about five feet tall, with a wrinkled face, little hair and crooked yellowed teeth. He had survived the cruelty of the Japanese occupation and the North Korean invasion. Kim was glad we were there. He wanted to help.

We gave him food, medicine and candy to take home and share with others. He did odd jobs around the base. I don't know where he lived. He had learned some English and could communicate, to a degree.

When the weather turned from brutally hot to frigid winter, I found him a discarded fatigue jacket. It was too big but he wore it with pride. It kept him warm.

One day I sat on a crude wooden bench writing a letter to my parents. Kim came in. "You have desk at home?" he asked in his soft, broken English.

"I do."

A gift unexpected

"You have name on desk?"

"No, just a desk."

"Please, write down name."

I took a piece of stationery and wrote, L.J. Adreon, and asked why he wanted it.

He smiled that crooked smile, "You'll see."

The conversation ended. I had to get back to duty.

Our company was scheduled to rotate back to the 38th Parallel. I was never anxious to return to combat. However, some of my buddies wanted to get back in action.

They reminded me of the guys on the USS Meigs, the gung-ho Marines who'd be cleaning their M1s and saying how they "couldn't wait to get a gook in their sights."

I was not anxious to get anyone in my sights. I was 25 years old, and older than most of those gung-ho guys, maybe by four or six years.

I've heard Marines first used the term "gook" in the early 20th Century in the Philippines. It's unfortunate we have to dehumanize our enemies with labels like gook, "jap", "kraut", and "chink".

Most South Koreans I met were good and kind people. My granddaughter married a Korean American, a terrific guy in every way.

So was Kim. He came to wish me luck every time we headed north.

After he asked my name, we headed to the 38th for 10 hard and sad days. We took a difficult hill with Chinese firing on us relentlessly. They also barraged our route with mortars

129

amid a cold, hard, almost freezing rain. We crawled in our small, alternating fireteams, water cascading down the hill throwing muddy water in our faces.

We fired toward flashes that revealed entrenched Chinese.

It took hours of inching our way close to the top. The air filled with smoke and the acrid odor of mortars and gunpowder. Rounds hit two of my buddies, Rick and Dave. I gave them morphine and stopped the bleeding. Others took them down the hill as I continued on with my platoon.

After many hours and too much blood we won the top. The same horrific scene, with rain washed bodies soaked in blood. The other corpsmen and I helped the wounded as best we could, but our morphine supply was limited. We took care to not exhaust it.

Then we dug in and held our position for days before we finally made it back to the battalion aid station.

Kim was in his usual Korean squat to greet me with his smile. I was sad and exhausted. Rick was dead. Dave survived but lost an eye and, maybe an arm. A copter evacuated him to the hospital ship, that ship I could've served on called "Repose." Like so many others, his fate is unknown to me.

Kim found me on my bunk. I must have looked bad. "You ok?" he asked.

I shrugged my shoulders.

"Can I call you LJ?"

"Sure, why not."

"You got beat out there?"

"No."

A gift unexpected

"Why so sad?"

"My friend Rick is dead, Dave and others badly hurt."

"So sorry, maybe I make you feel a little better."

He opened a paper bag and took out a small triangle of wood painted black. On it, in what looked like Mother of Pearl, was inscribed my name, L J Adreon.

"You put on your home desk. Maybe, you remember me. I hope you like. I made it."

My eyes grew misty. I needed this. I reached out to him. We hugged.

All I could say was, "Thank you."

25

Last liberty
Korea, 1951

Eighteen days of ocean monotony finally gave way to an island in the distance. We knew how Columbus felt when he first spotted America.

He thought he'd found Japan. He was looking at Cuba. We found Japan on the way across the Pacific, as the Meigs pulled into the harbor at Yokohama.

After a brief stop to pick up supplies, the ship headed for the port of Kobe. We'd get our last liberty there before heading to Korea. Five thousand Marines descended on the city.

Five years after beating Japan, I didn't know what welcome we'd get from our former enemy. It was more than cordial. Hundreds of young Japanese women waited at the bottom of the gangplanks as eager Marines began their last night of pre-Korean freedom.

It was warm and sultry. Two of my buddies, Darry and Marshall, and I decided to split away from the mad scramble of boots hitting the Japanese dock. We didn't have an appetite for the drinking and carousing that many Marines sought, with their attitude of "Go for it, for tomorrow we're at war." We all shared foreboding at what was to come.

Darry had heard of a restaurant at the top of a hill inside a hotel. We could take a fresh shower, relax and get a good meal.

We were astonished to discover that Russians operated the restaurant. My vision of an exotic meal of raw fish and sticky rice went unrealized.

Once assured the room had a good shower, we paid up and each took a long, hot, fresh water shower with Japanese liquid soap. We then headed to the restaurant. We ordered wine selected by Marshall, who seemed to know something about it.

Several things about the restaurant seemed odd. Because it was hot in the room, two young women with huge fans stood beside the table and fanned us. And the waiter told us to raise our hand when we wanted something. He then stayed out of sight behind a partition, observing in mirrors—his way of allowing us privacy.

After the meal, which was unremarkable, we walked around the mostly residential area, stopping at a local bar for a beer, and headed back to the ship.

Small-to-medium-size hotels dominated the area around the port in Kobe, which appeared relatively undamaged by the war. Starting about 10 p.m., the Shore Patrol began rounding up Marines, who were expected at the ship no later than midnight.

The port boomed with our visit. I'm sure the hotels enjoyed an occupancy rate of at least 300%, as Marines rented the rooms by the hour.

At midnight, the deck of the Meigs filled with Marines in disarray after the self-imposed abuse of a last-fling liberty. The air stank of whiskey mixed with stale cigarette smoke.

26

Stench to stalemate
Korea, 1951

A few days later, the smells had changed, but not for the better. We arrived in Korea in the spring of 1951. No spring had smelled like the port city of Pusan.

When we landed, the city lay in shambles, buildings destroyed, debris covering the streets, disheveled men, women and children scurrying about with no apparent purpose.

I didn't anticipate the sickening, vile stench of Pusan. It was the odor of many toilets. Fighting had destroyed the sanitary systems. Raw sewage ran in the streets.

Fortunately, we didn't have to endure Pusan for long. Rows of trucks waited for us.

We'd come off the USS Meigs, nervous but glad to be past the endless monotony of 18 days at sea.

Military trucks had assembled at the port of Pusan awaiting our arrival. We loaded aboard the military trucks and convoyed to an air strip outside the city. The strip contained acres of helicopters, an amazing sight.

We separated into groups for each copter. I had no idea they could hold so many men—there must've been 10 to 15 on each.

We sat in rows, each of us handed a parachute. Then someone helped us put it on. "It's simple, when you jump, be sure you clear the plane," a gruff voice said.

He said to count to 10, reach down, pull the cord and the chute would open, letting me float down. After hitting the ground, I should hit a solid piece sitting in the center of the chute to dislodge it.

"That's all there is to it."

He moved on. I sat there, stunned. When we jump? Me, jump? That wasn't part of our training.

The copter took off. We flew low. The copter rattled with noise, shaking and wobbling through the air. Ventilation was excessive as air leaked in from all directions.

I did manage to get a look at the Korean landscape. Rice paddies tucked in everywhere, even on hillsides. They looked like swamps with green things growing out of the water.

As we went north, the rolling hills and valleys became mountains and crevices. I saw cities along the way, more like villages, but I couldn't see any detail.

Happily, nothing happened to the copter. No one shot at us. The parachute stayed packed. Finally, after a forever flight, we landed smoothly at an airstrip near a little town called Inji.

Stench to stalemate

Inji wasn't far from the 38th Parallel, where the front line had sort of settled. After a year of sweeps north and south, up and down the peninsula, armies faced off along the 38th into a hill-by-hill warfare.

A commander addressed us before we got onto waiting trucks. He explained it was the mission of the First Marine Division to take and hold the high ground. We were to kill and wound as many of the enemy as possible. But the impetus to win had changed to more of a holding action along the 38th Parallel.

It seemed that neither side expected to conquer territory, just to hold where the battle lines had settled at the 38th. The objective was to cause enough casualties to force a negotiated ceasefire. This was the spring of 1951. Actual peace talks started in July at a place called Panmunjom. The ceasefire didn't come until two years later in July of 1953.

I'd crossed an ocean to fight in a stalemate. A deadly, years-long stalemate.

A Korean man on the streets of Seoul (National Archives)

27

Korean kindness
Korea, 1951

Stalemate in the broader sense. But the front line moved enough that if we weren't on it, we couldn't be sure where it was.

That terrified me when I got lost once, stumbling through thick foliage that attacked me with thorns. I couldn't find my unit. We had scattered when hit by a sudden bombardment. I felt alone and increasingly disoriented.

Better get back to the main road. But I turned the wrong way and wandered deeper into the woods. I frantically rushed in one direction, then another, getting nowhere.

Somewhere nearby was the front. That meant Chinese. I had to avoid them.

Breaking into a small opening, I recognized a narrow road. I walked the road as quickly as I could, ending in a village that I knew from an earlier patrol.

Completely exhausted, I sat on the roadside. I don't know how long I sat, looking disheveled, dirty and bleeding from the thorns.

Then I looked up to see a thin, old, fragile-looking Korean man standing over me. He signaled for me to follow. I struggled to my feet. We walked a few steps to his hut.

Inside, two wrinkled women filled a water bucket and washed the dirt and blood from my flesh and clothes. It felt good. I nodded my thanks.

The man came back carrying several large bowls with rice and vegetables. We sat in a semi-circle and passed the bowls between us. I was famished.

We'd been told not to eat the local food, but I shoveled rice into my mouth. It was to be my only Korean family meal.

After eating, I stretched out on a straw mat and fell fast asleep. The sun had nearly set when I awoke. I knew I had to get back to my unit.

I got up, mouthed the words, "thank you" to the Korean family. I respectfully bowed to them. They returned the bow. Smiles were exchanged. I left the hut feeling refreshed and grateful, and knew the road would take me back to the base.

Night had settled in before I arrived back at the base, where my company had returned after the attack. "What the hell happened to you?" blurted out my fellow corpsman, Sam.

I explained my disorientation and how I lacked any sense of direction. I added that whenever I stayed in a hotel

Korean kindness

Even in war, kindness.

and left the room to go to the elevator, I inevitably turned in the wrong way.

He said officers ordered the company back to base right after the artillery attack. "I felt bad leaving without you."

They'd looked for me, and told the lieutenant I was missing, but he said they had to leave.

It didn't matter now. I was lost. I was found. And I'd experienced the kindness of more Koreans, this time a poor family in a no-name village.

28

City of orphans
Korea, 1952

Not that all South Koreans were friendly: Down an alley in Seoul, we saw a group of seven bedraggled and unwashed children. Turning around, another group approached from behind. All carried what looked like baseball bats.

Instinctively, we pulled the weapons from our shoulders. We walked slowly ahead toward the group of seven while the others followed us. They stood their ground. We stopped, shouted and gestured for them to get out of the way.

Early that morning, Dr. Koz had ordered me to deliver documents to a Seoul hospital. He suggested I take some of my platoon for protection.

The main road to Seoul felt haphazardly patched. I enjoyed driving as our rugged Jeep bounced to the capital city. It was a nice break from the routines at the receiving tent.

The war had left Seoul a damaged city. Shells had blasted building after building into empty spaces. Few buildings had any unbroken glass, Debris was piled on the sidewalks. It looked like the pictures of Berlin after World War II.

Still, the city bristled with activity, both civilian and military.

Shortly after entering the city's perimeter we encountered a wooden gate guarded by the Army. Two soldiers asked us to identify ourselves. I thought that odd since we were Marines driving a Marine Corps Jeep.

They insisted on seeing our dog tags, then took our medical papers and said they would deliver them to the hospital. They explained the precautions arose from an incident where men dressed as South Korean soldiers had tried to plant bombs at Army installations.

We had time to spare, so we asked if we could drive in and see the city. They told us how to find the main downtown area.

I parked on the street. We wanted to stretch our legs and take a walk around what we thought was downtown Seoul.

We passed a fruit stand with luscious, shiny apples. We tried to explain to the little old Korean man that we were not allowed to eat any of the local food. He pleaded for us to buy an apple. We bought one and, after walking around the corner, gave it to two kids playing the Korean version of hopscotch.

When we rounded the next corner, we found ourselves caught between the menacing kids. Some looked high school age, others younger than 10. They all wore torn military outfits.

We'd stopped and waited. They stared. "Weapons up," shouted our sergeant. Two rifles aimed at the front group and

City of orphans

two at those behind us. He then told us to continue walking toward the group of seven. Suddenly, both groups turned and ran.

As we drove out of town, we stopped at the gate to ask what that was all about. The soldiers explained gangs of kids filled Seoul, war orphans who preyed on the vulnerable. They chuckled that four armed Marines might appear a target.

Driving back to the base, I fretted about the orphan ambush. Would we have fired and killed little orphans? Thank God, they ran away.

I did no more sightseeing in Korea.

Seoul, 1952

29

Trench trauma
Korea, winter 1951/1952

We had driven the Chinese from the hill. Just another day at the 38th Parallel in Korea in early winter. Our lieutenant signaled for our platoon to gather for new orders. He was a seasoned Marine, well respected by all of us. He had led us in many battles.

A man of few words, he spoke quickly with a loud voice over the sounds of nearby exploding shells. He said he needed six riflemen and one corpsman to go through the trench, determine if any enemy is left, and take what action is required. "If there are Chinese in the trench, they will ambush you if they can," he said. "We need to secure the main trench and any side trenches. Who's willing to go?"

About ten Marines raised their hands. The Lieutenant picked six. "I also need a corpsman." He looked at me and at Sammy, the only corpsmen of our platoon.

Trench trauma

Sammy had just come back from cleaning out foxholes. I knew it was my turn to volunteer. I raised my hand. The lieutenant nodded and said, "Ok, we're set. Follow me." On the way he cautioned us to watch for booby traps and to move quietly to avoid detection by any Chinese.

The trench was about six-feet deep and rarely wide enough for two guys to walk next to each other. Some places it narrowed and turned to follow the contour of the hilltop. It was twilight on the mountain. The trench was dark. We carried our small flashlights. Our gunnery sergeant led the group. I followed behind the sixth guy. It was slow going. The footing was treacherous; the mud sucked at our boots.

The trench's length surprised me. About 40 minutes in, we found three bodies of Chinese soldiers lying in the mud. I checked them to be sure they were dead. I did not move them because we feared booby traps. We climbed over and continued.

The trench took an abrupt turn to the left where other trenches branched off to either side. Suddenly, I heard the staccato sound of heavy, Russian-made, rapid-fire burp guns unloading with flashes of light and smoke from our right. Three Marines went down. I took my .45 out of the holster and moved toward the action. The Marines fired their M1's into that side trench, moving forward as the Chinese retreated.

I arrived at the intersection and, glancing, thought I saw movement to the left. I dropped down, crawled into that other narrow, dark dugout. Didn't see anything more; crawled in deeper. Two Chinese appeared and began raising their machine guns, which were awkward heavy weapons in that tight space. Before they got them lifted, I rapidly fired seven rounds, holding the pistol with both hands. They screamed. I heard them fall. My flashlight verified they were down.

I quickly turned and returned to the main trench. It was quiet. I checked the prone Marines and couldn't get a pulse on two. The third was breathing with blood spewing from his gut. I cut away his jacket and applied pressure to stop the bleeding. He twisted and writhed in pain. I gave him a shot of morphine. The bleeding stopped. The other three Marines came out of the side trench. I went in behind them to check on the Chinese, finding four in the mud, all dead. I went back into the left-side trench and verified that my handgun had done its job.

We were only steps from the trench's end. We immobilized the wounded Marine, and carried him as we headed back the way we came. Two Marines dead, one badly wounded, six Chinese dead. Mission over.

The lieutenant greeted us as we emerged from the entrance. He shook his head and said, "You guys did a good job. Those Chinks were hiding to come after us during the night."

Good job, the lieutenant said, but I felt disgusted and queasy. Sammy and I went back into the trench with stretcher bearers to recover the dead Marines. Others carried the wounded Marine down to the forward aid station at the bottom of the hill to be treated by the doctor on duty.

Trench trauma

Later, I learned the wounded Marine was coptered to the hospital ship and recovered enough to go home. His war ended in that trench, as it had for eight other souls.

30

Dodging a bullet
Korea, winter 1951/1952

The Chinese carried better arms for their ambushes, particularly the Burp Gun that could fire 900 rounds in only a minute.

One of their cold-blooded ambushes came after the weather got cold, after the hot, sticky, mosquito-filled days of summer had given way to Korean winter.

The battalion had issued us green woolen trousers, cotton long johns, an undershirt, a wool top shirt and a calf-length, lined, hooded parka. Our new wool caps added ear flaps under our helmets. Cleated boots came with special breathable socks. Our gloves covered mittens. We cut holes in our mittens and gloves for our trigger finger. The cold, wet winds would find weather-ready troops.

We'd guarded a relatively small hill for about nine days under continuously falling snow. During the day, we'd build

small fires to warm our C rations, melt ice in our canteens and dry our socks. We huddled around fires as the icy wind swept over the hilltop. Replacements coming soon would get us out of the cold and back to base.

In the late afternoon, trucks carrying our replacements started up the curving narrow road. They moved like turtles through the slippery, relentless snow. We waited. We watched. Day's last light faded into darkness. We still waited.

The hillside suddenly erupted with explosions, the rapid firing of automatic weapons, and the whistles and bugles of battle. Chinese on both sides of the snow-filled road had ambushed our replacements. Orders came to leave foxholes and barricades and move toward the battle. Our buddies needed help.

We followed the flashes of light, smoke and noise. Slipping and sliding, we worked our way down the frozen sludge. When we got closer, we could see an explosion had overturned the convoy's lead truck, blocking the road.

The Chinese wore their white, quilted jackets. The jackets were reversible, white for snow conditions and a dingy yellow for others.

At least the snow jackets made the Chinese easier to distinguish as the enemy. When in firing range, we started shooting at the white jackets. Our platoon of about 40 men led the rest of our company. We let loose with all our firepower.

Our Browning automatics proved devastating. The Marine sharpshooters fired clip after clip from their M1s. As we got closer, I held my carbine's trigger to fire round after round at the white jackets.

After about an hour of furious battle, the tide turned and the Chinese began disappearing into the hillside. The smell at the roadside was a powerful mix of sour smoke and pungent garlic. The Chinese apparently ate garlic to fend off colds.

We searched for wounded amid a scattering of shots from the retreating Chinese. The ambush had ended. We worked through the night but not until the morning's first light could we see all the damage.

Blood was everywhere, on the road, in the trucks, and on the hill. Bodies of our men and white-jacketed Chinese lay scattered hundreds of feet down the road. Some Marines didn't make it out of their trucks.

I could only speculate if any of my bullets had contributed to that night's destruction of young life. I'm haunted by the image of a young Chinese soldier with a white jacket covered with frozen, black blood. I'm more haunted by the bloodied bodies of my fellow Marines who were caught up in the ambush.

We did our best to stop the bleeding of our wounded. I ran out of morphine before dawn. Our lieutenant had radioed the base for help. It would be about 24 hours before another company could make it.

With little rest, we stabilized the situation. We readied the wounded for evacuation. We laid dead Marines inside the trucks. After we had taken care of all the Marines, we treated wounded Chinese, now prisoners. Marines piled dead Chinese on the road's edge for later burial. It would require heavier equipment than we had to penetrate the frozen ground.

I remembered the classroom back at Pendleton when guys dressed as Chinese came in and opened fire causing us

Dodging a bullet

to dive under our desks. That message of always being on the alert resonated on that icy hill.

My company could have been the victim of the ambush. We dodged a bullet that night.

31

To the 38th
Korea, 1951

Before I knew the horrors of combat, when I was fresh off the boat, the helicopters had dropped us near battalion headquarters. There, Marines in camouflage called names from clipboard lists. Mine came early. (The alphabet!)

My gear strapped to my back, my carbine slung over my shoulder, I joined a group boarding a truck. Trucks would become familiar transportation in the months to come.

We arrived at our battalion's sprawling tent city in a pounding rain. We now were close to the 38th Parallel where the war raged among the mountains.

The damp penetrated my combat gear as I climbed off the truck. The rain sounded like drumsticks beating on my helmet.

My cot sat in the middle of the tent. It was OK, but not the Sleep Number mattresses of today. We slept under mosquito netting during the spring and the summer seasons.

At night, we could hear the noise of small running feet above. Rats infested the camp and toured our tent nightly along the horizontal wood supports above. To fight them, we'd put something called Warfarin in small jars on the flat wood. The idea was that the rats would drink the blood thinner and go wherever rats go to slowly bleed to death.

I don't know how well it worked. Rats, or their friends, or relatives or neighbors kept coming back. Sometimes they died in our tent and some poor guy would wake to a dead rat in the netting above. Not nice, but experiences in Korea only got worse.

It took us six days or so to get settled and assigned our duty at the aid station. I was ordered to work with a doctor in the receiving tent. That's when I met Doc Koz.

Stretchers brought in wounded Marines and Koz, as we called him, assessed wounds and decided on treatment. I'd assist him and make sure stretchers got the Marine to the right tent for treatment.

For wounds we couldn't handle at the aid station, helicopters transported Marines to a field hospital further south, or to a hospital ship off the coast. I think we called the full-service field hospital Easy Med. I have no idea why. There was nothing easy about it. Most times, we'd drive the wounded to Easy Med by Jeep or in a truck-like ambulance called a Cracker Boxer.

To the 38th

We rotated between the front at the 38th Parallel and the battalion station. Because time at the front was intense, we needed time at the station to recover. The rotation didn't always work precisely.

Our first trip to the front came about 12 days after we'd arrived at the battalion camp. We carried special backpacks designed for what we'd face. We had our weapons in top condition with plenty of ammo. The trucks carried us over the bumpy road we called the MSR, or Main Service Road, to relieve Marines at the 38th.

The first time we felt lucky as the sun broke through the usual grey sky. We arrived at the base of a medium-sized hill, maybe 2,500 feet high, in a forest that looked wrecked as if a forest fire had swept through. The terrain looked rocky but this time, only moderately steep.

The Chinese held the high ground. Most of the hills had numbers. So many hills, the numbers ran together. I think the numbers had something to do with a hill's height in meters.

We'd waste no time, with our ascent to start at dawn.

We stuck together as a platoon, with our fire teams of four men, two with rifles and two toting a Browning automatic and its ammo. Fire teams cherished their Browning which could determine their fate. The Browning packed much more punch than a rifleman's M1. It weighed about 20 pounds and came with a tripod or bipod, compared to the 12 pounds of an M1. It could fire 500 to 650 rounds per minute and was effective for a distance of up to 1500 yards.

I carried the carbine I'd learned to shoot back at Camp Pendleton. It was lighter and less powerful than other rifles in the field. Although not accurate, the rifle could fire 30 continuous rounds by holding the trigger, which I did many times in the months to come.

Veterans told us to aim the carbine at faces because its rounds might not penetrate the padded jackets worn by the Chinese. The vision of bullets exploding in a face, even the face of the enemy, horrified me. However, we had orders to obey.

Most of the time, we didn't get close enough to aim for the face. But when we did, we tried our best to hit the enemy. It was about survival.

With the three fire teams in a squad led by a corporal, and a platoon's three squads led by a second lieutenant, each platoon added up to about 40 or 45 men. Two corpsmen went with each platoon, or about one corpsman per 20 men.

I was assigned to the 2nd platoon of Dog Company, and each company had about 235 men, including corpsmen, radiomen and other specialists..

The officer back at Camp Pendleton was right about focusing on my platoon and company. Confusion reigned in combat, making survival the focus. I learned to listen intently for the lieutenant's voice shouting at the 2nd platoon.

When those orders came, they were something like, "Second platoon move out, split left." It sounded like a football play called by the quarterback in a huddle.

At first light, we started up the hill.

Confusion and Consequences

32

Mistakes happen
Korea, 1951

We took one small hill without a battle. To our surprise, the Chinese had left. We all breathed a sigh of relief.

Until our dive bombers roared overhead.

Earlier, my Dog Company gathered on a crystal-clear evening at the base of the short hill, maybe only 1,500-to-2,000 feet high. "Tomorrow will be a perfect day to recapture this hill," said our soft-spoken captain.

He explained that around dawn, our artillery and mortars would blast the hilltop. He'd also called for air support, which should arrive shortly after we'd start climbing.

"Get ready," he said. "This should be a fast and successful operation."

The Corsair air support meant the task should be easier and safer. Nonetheless, I and the other corpsman in our platoon, Sammy, made sure we had all our gear ready.

Just before the sun came up, we heard the artillery and mortar attacks and saw them light up the hilltop. "Second platoon, move up!" our platoon lieutenant shouted.

We began our climb. The Chinese appeared hunkered down. We moved fast. We heard the barrage stop and saw the Corsairs fly over and drop their loads. We could sense this attack would be a "piece of cake" compared to the usual assaults. The Chinese still weren't shooting.

Our climb went straight up. No leapfrogging. No crawling. We found the Chinese machine gun nests empty. We met no resistance as we approached the top in record time.

The order came to stop to ensure the Corsairs had finished. The hill grew quiet. "Take the hilltop," the lieutenant ordered.

We methodically moved up the remaining short distance. No resistance. The Chinese had left.

Suddenly, dive-bombers roared overhead.

They dove to just 25 feet above the hill to drop their deadly napalm. In seconds, they swept across, turned their bombs loose and disappeared into a smoke-filled sky.

Horrified, Sammy and I, at the rear of our platoon, realized the bombers had attacked our men. The pilots didn't know the Chinese had abandoned the hill. Their deadly bombs spewed orange and yellow flames. The hill was alive

Mistakes happen

with frantic Marines on fire. Our lieutenant radioed to stop the planes.

Too late; damage done.

Sammy and I and other corpsmen rushed from one burn victim to another. We'd not before dealt with the charred, waxen skin of napalm victims.

Some Marines had third-degree or fourth-degree burns over 80% or more of their bodies. They wouldn't survive. We loaded them with morphine to alleviate the all-consuming pain. We found others with less-extensive burns and tried our best to relieve their pain and cover the burns with ointment and bandages.

In the most severe cases, we started an IV, which we knew was protocol for burn victims. As fast as possible, we sent them on stretchers down to the forward aid station for more advanced treatment.

Our lieutenant called for medevac copters to take the wounded to hospital camps or ships. His message was desperate. Treatment speed meant life and death.

We shook our heads at what napalm does to its victims. This time, our napalm to our men. We knew survivors faced painful skin grafts and unbelievable misery. Maybe, they could recover after months or years to a relatively normal life with a face or body that might never look right.

I asked the lieutenant how it happened. "Air support had been ordered to hit the Chinese at the hilltop," he said. "The Corsairs did the job."

He hesitated and sighed, "We thought the air bombardment was over. I ordered the men to take the hilltop. It all happened in seconds."

I could see the pain and anguish in his eyes. He could see my exhaustion and despair.

"Adreon, this is war." He shrugged. "Mistakes happen."

33

A blown trip to Seoul
Korea, winter 1952

The extreme cold had swept in from the North. I mean bitter cold. Temperatures hovered below zero with a fierce wind. We covered ourselves to prevent the wind from attacking our flesh. However, a good result was a slowdown in the fighting intensity. It was just too damn cold with too much ice and snow to try to climb a hill.

Doc Koz came to me early one slow morning in the Battalion Aid Station tent and said, "Adreon, we need to make another trip to Seoul. You handled the last trip and know the way."

He explained they were sending two Marines to the hospital there and needed paperwork delivered. I'd need to take the two guys and a rifleman with me in the early morning.

He could see the frown on my face and asked, "Why the face? You have a problem? You told me once that you liked driving the jeep."

I took a deep breath, "Doc, I'd rather you send someone else this time. I found Seoul depressing."

He shook his head, "I don't have anyone else that I can send. If you don't volunteer, I'll be forced to order you to take the jeep."

I smirked and said, "OK, I volunteer."

We met the next morning at about 0600. It was still dark, but the wind had let up and conditions were tolerable. I was introduced to a Marine private first class named Tom from another platoon and the two patients named Elmer and Lou. We were given special cold-weather gear including something like a ski mask to protect our faces. We were assured that the road had been checked by engineers and was safe.

The jeep had been fitted so two people could sit uncomfortably in the back and two in the front. No weapons on the vehicle. It was probably the same one I'd driven before.

Tom sat with me in the front and Elmer and Lou in the back. Both had head bandages but seemed OK. Doc Koz told us they would not need medical treatment on the trip. They were going to the hospital for some tests.

The road was in better shape than it was on my earlier trip. Some of the shell holes had been filled and, consequently, the trip would not be as rough. It also meant that we could go faster and make the trip in less time. I was anxious to get it over with.

A couple hours in, Elmer asked me to stop as soon as I could because he had to go. I found a wider portion of the road, pulled over for our pit stop. We took turns and did our

A blown trip to Seoul

best to keep the exposure to the cold at a minimum. Urinating under those conditions is something I wouldn't want to do very often.

Back in the jeep, we made good time. There was no traffic on the road in either direction. I thought that unusual. We came to an abrupt turn in the road that I didn't remember from the previous trip. Slowed down where the road narrowed at the turn. I thought that was also odd.

Suddenly, a blinding blast of light, a shattering explosion, the jeep lifted into the air landing in a gulley alongside the road. It flipped over but ended upright. I was holding onto the wheel and did not get thrown out of the vehicle. Tom, Elmer and Lou were gone. My head had hit the windshield. I felt blood trickling down from my forehead, my vision blurred. I was shaking. I opened my med kit, took out some bandages and held them tight against my forehead. In a few minutes the bleeding stopped. I stopped shaking. My vision slowly cleared. I thought, *what a lucky SOB am I.*

As soon as I was able to breathe again, I climbed out to search for the others. I found Elmer against a boulder, not moving. I checked for a pulse. No pulse and he wasn't breathing. Elmer was dead.

Several yards away, Lou was face down on a patch of ice. I turned him over, saw that he was breathing and quickly assessed his condition. His face was frozen in a tense expression, his eyes closed. I tried to sit him up, to open his eyes. I shouted his name pleading with him to talk. In a few minutes his whole body went limp. I checked for a pulse.

None. He was gone. I could see that he was only a kid, maybe 18 years old, another sad moment in this war.

I searched through the slushy ice for Tom. Couldn't find him. Where in the hell was he? I started back to the jeep. He was on the ground next to the front wheel, his jacket half torn from his body, his knees bloody from crawling back to the vehicle. His face streaked with blood. I used a clean bandage and some alcohol and wiped the blood from his face. He looked up at me and said, "I'm OK, just cut up a bit. Where is Elmer?, Lou?"

I shook my head. "Both dead."

I grabbed Tom under his shoulders and helped him up. He was able to climb back into the jeep. I sat in the driver's side, trying to figure out what we could do. I turned on the ignition and the motor started, to our surprise. We knew we couldn't drive the vehicle out of the ice-filled gulley. We let the motor run to warm us up. Tom checked the radio, which was working. He called the Battalion Aid Station and requested they send an ambulance. We were close to Seoul on the main service road. All we had to do was wait, which we did for about two hours, turning the motor off and on to keep warm.

The truck ambulance arrived. We directed the driver to the two bodies. After we loaded them on the ambulance, he drove us to Seoul where I delivered the packet of papers to the hospital. We hitched a ride on a truck headed back to our battalion base. Tom and I lifted the two Marines into the back of the truck.

We arrived back at our base that night, and were dropped

A blown trip to Seoul

off at the aid station. The dead Marines were taken from the truck and placed in the transport pick-up area with other corpses to be taken south where they'd be shipped back to the states. Tom stayed at the aid station to be examined and treated. I never saw him again.

I felt weak and totally wiped out. I slowly walked to my tent and staggered to my bunk. I didn't try to change my filthy clothes. I just crashed.

Adreon stops in Tokyo, awaiting flight to San Francisco.

34

What took so long?
Korea, 1952

Back at the battalion station, I was in the receiving tent when a Marine handed papers to Doc Koz. He glanced at them and called me over.

I will forever remember his words: "Adreon, get your gear, you're going south."

I'd leave within 48 hours, headed for the First Marine Division headquarters in Masan, a city on the south coast of Korea. There, I'd get a new assignment.

Magic words, "Going south." Everyone wanted to go south, away from the 38th Parallel, away from the foxholes.

I asked Doc Koz to explain. He shrugged. Then something nice: Doc Koz said he'd miss me and my excellent work. We shook hands. It was our final goodbye. I hope he made it home OK.

Over the next two days, I said goodbyes to my platoon and the Koreans who worked at the base. Good friends met me at the helicopter pad on departure day, several of them scheduled to leave soon themselves.

We agreed we'd put the war behind us. We felt it best to forget Korea, which also meant our friendship was over. Watching them wave as the helicopter took off was the last I saw of my Marine buddies.

I looked down somewhat confused by the sudden order, though cheered that they waved and yelled for me as the copter lifted off.

We landed at an airfield just in time for lunch. I then caught a ride on a truck for the short trip to Masan, where I was ushered into a small office. The weathered face of a Marine major peered at me from behind a steel-gray desk.

He surprised me by standing up, walking over, holding out his hand and uttering, "Congratulations." He gestured to me to sit in front of his desk. He took a seat in a chair next to mine.

"Adreon, you have orders to report to the Naval Officer Candidate School at Newport, Rhode Island," he said.

They'd assigned me a priority so I could start with the next class in about 30 days. It was a 90-day course after which I'd be commissioned an ensign.

I had to chuckle. It had taken the Navy more than a year to approve my application. The major explained that I'd board a ship at Pusan, 20 miles away, head to Tokyo and then fly to San Francisco where I'd report to the Navy's personnel office.

What took so long?

I asked what to take with me. "Take your clothes and personal items, no weapons."

In Tokyo, that priority flight kept me waiting eight days. I could leave the ship but had to check in every four hours. I found a little art shop near Ginza, the main shopping street. It's there that I bought the little figurines that reminded me of village Koreans, and that now sit on a shelf above my den TV.

Tokyo teemed with little cars honking at each other. It seemed the horn had replaced the brake. I visited the Emperor's Palace, an Asian-style building surrounded by a moat, though I couldn't enter the grounds.

Adreon at the Emperor's Palace moat.

One day, I sat on a bench at Tokyo University and people watched. Two women students smiled and one, carrying several books, said "Hi." I was surprised they were fluent in English.

After a bit of chit chat, I asked how they felt about American servicemen.

They said they didn't buy the government's propaganda that blamed the United States. "The war was a horrible mistake by a greedy Japanese government and allowed by an Emperor who had no guts and no power," one of the girls said. "How do you feel about us?"

I had to think before answering. I remembered movies showing cruel Japanese faces as they destroyed Americans. I recalled my Korean friend telling how the Japanese occupiers had mistreated his people. I also knew that we killed and maimed hundreds of thousands of innocent civilians in Nagasaki and Hiroshima.

I finally answered as best I could: "I agree that the war was a futile power grab with devastating effects on your people and Americans."

I told them it'd been over for seven years, and that I didn't dislike them because they were Japanese.

"I don't know you," I said. "Eventually, I think we all will judge each other for who we are."

They smiled and offered to show me around. We spent a delightful hour together. They introduced me to one of their teachers who'd been in the Japanese Navy, who also seemed friendly.

What took so long?

The tour over, we shook hands and wished each other good luck.

I had seen enough of Japan. I was anxious to head for home.

35

Confusion in San Francisco

California, 1952

Finally, I was ordered back to the ship because my flight was ready.

At the airport, my duffle bag was inspected and I discovered that my medkits were gone. I'd emptied my medkits when leaving Korea, replacing the supplies with my Argus C3 camera and film canisters of film. I had taken pictures in Korea of villages, my friend Kim, and buddies at the battalion base. There were no combat pictures because we didn't take cameras to the 38th.

I fumed that someone would take my camera and film. I'm still sorry I don't have pictures of Marines I served with, and especially Darry, my best friend who was killed months after we'd arrived.

My flight stopped at Guam and Midway Island on our way to Honolulu. I had time to walk near the airfield on Midway and watched the large, funny-looking birds dance in the sand. We called them Gooney Birds. I later learned they were Black Footed Albatrosses.

After a change of planes in Honolulu, we landed in San Francisco. Sunshine reflecting off the Golden Gate Bridge thrilled me after the dreary gray of Korea. I reported to the Naval personnel office.

An officer reviewed my file and said something that astounded me, that Congress had recently limited how long a reservist must serve on active duty. "I think you're eligible for release in about three or four months."

"But what if I become an officer?"

"That would add four more years of active duty, and eight in the reserve."

I called home and talked to my dad. His response was quick and firm. He said, "Why are we even talking about this? You'll be an officer and never in a foxhole again."

I complained that, at 26 years old, I wouldn't get out of the Navy until I was 30. Still, he wanted me to go for it. I didn't have a job waiting, and faced a shortage of jobs.

"This is a once-in-a-lifetime opportunity," he said, adding that it'd be good for my resume and most important, I'd be safe.

Spending another four years in the Navy sounded dismal to a young man wanting to get on with his life. But Dad

pushed it: "Being an officer in the Navy is a lot different than what you've known as an enlisted man."

He also figured that if I didn't take the commission, I'd be sent back to Korea.

The next day, I boarded a plane with my mind a muddle.

36

Smoking kills
Korea, 1952

The flickering flame of a Zippo lighter penetrated the night. It was so dark I couldn't see anyone in the foxhole. A yell pierced the night as the butt of the rifle struck its target.

The flame went out. No words were spoken.

Amid shivering cold and gusts of wind, I helped the guy who'd yelled, a Marine named Jerry. I pressed his head where blood gushed, feeling warm as it thickened in the cold air. The compression stopped the flow as he cursed.

I gave him a shot of morphine to ease the pain. With the first light, we put him on a stretcher and sent him down the hill.

• • •

We spent 10 days at the front and then rotated back to base camp. Jerry was OK and after another 10 days or so, joined us as we headed back to the 38th, where we quickly took a hill.

Jerry was tough, agile and strong, as good a Marine as any. When we secured the hill, he seemed delighted to see enemy bodies. I found the sight disturbing and sad. We dug in for the night.

We'd lost five men that day. Mortar shells started landing in what was another black night. Tension filled the air. Jerry did it again—the Zippo flamed.

This time, two shots rang out. The smell of burnt flesh filled the foxhole. I checked for a pulse. Jerry was dead.

• • •

An inquiry at the battalion base summoned me to testify. Three officers asked questions.

"Adreon, you were the Corpsman who treated him at the first incident. What did he say?"

"He asked me who hit him. I told him I didn't know. He said he'd get that son of a bitch and put him in a ditch. I reminded him of rules against smoking in the foxhole. Jerry said something like, 'Fuck the rules. All my life I've been told what to do and what to say.' He went on about his DI (drill instructor) being a retard who didn't know shit, that our lieutenant was a dumb-ass, and that he was smarter, stronger and faster than all of 'em. I remember him saying, 'I'm gonna smoke whenever and wherever I want to and the next gung-ho bastard who tries to stop me better look out.'"

"Have you had conversations with him before the first incident?"

"Not really, but one day when we were all sitting around reading mail he burst out laughing and said, 'Hey guys, listen to this from my mom.' Jerry read something like, 'Son, I hope you've stopped smoking those vile cigarillos or whatever you call those things. Smoking will kill you.' He snarled. 'Here I am being shot at by gooks every fuckin' day and my stupid mom is worried about my smoking.'"

"You were also in the foxhole when he died. Who were the other Marines there?"

"I can't say. There were many nights, many foxholes. When mortars started falling we jumped into the closest foxhole. I guess Jerry and I jumped in together, but I don't know who else."

The Colonel frowned at my response and said they'd put a notice on the bulletin board about the inquiry and asked anyone with knowledge to come forward. No response. They called me because my name was on the medical report.

He then paused, took off his cap, ran his fingers through his slightly greying hair.

"Do I understand you heard only two shots?"

"Yeah, just two shots."

"Did you ask any of the other Marines in the foxhole what they saw?"

"No, I was busy tending to Jerry. Also, we had to remain silent during the night. At first light, I left the foxhole telling the Marines that someone would come get his body."

"Adreon, what do you think really happened the night he died?"

"I don't know. It was pitch black. I saw the Zippo flame up, heard shots, it was over in a second."

"Is it possible he could've been shot by an enemy who'd come up on the hole?"

I paused. The colonel's eyes told me that he knew the truth. A slight smile creased my face. "I guess that's possible."

• • •

Smoking kills

I'm sure Jerry's parents received the standard U.S. Marine Corps letter of appreciation for their son's ultimate sacrifice, killed in action in the service of his country in Korea in the winter of 1951.

Jerry's mom was right.

Smoking kills.

Naval Station Newport (U.S. Navy)

37

Dilemma at Newport
Rhode Island, 1952

The last of my many flights glided smoothly in for a landing at Newport, Rhode Island.

A shuttle took me to the base, along with sailors in pea coats and a group of civilians. I wore the only clothes I had, my Marine Corps everyday drab green uniform, a combat jacket and a cap with the Corps insignia.

At 0900 the next morning, we assembled in a paved area beside a one-story white frame building, the officer school's HQ. The school's commander stepped onto the front porch in splendid naval officer attire. He had a starched look with speckled gray hair showing under his cap's gold braid. Braids also shone on his dark blue jacket with dazzling ribbons on his lapel.

Ninety pair of eyes looked as he got the group's attention. Without changing expression, he began in a deep voice: "I welcome the new class of officer candidates."

He said we were a nice mix of fleet men and new recruits from colleges. The next three months would be intense as they made us into proud Navy officers.

Then something bizarre: He focused on me because, in my Marine Corps outfit, I stood out. "What uniform are you wearing?"

I answered, "United States Marine Corps."

"Are you on active duty in the Navy?"

"Yes sir."

"How long have you been in the Navy?"

Quickly adding my time during WWII plus this tour, I answered, "More than 30 months."

He bellowed, "You need to be in a Navy uniform to conform to our school regulations. You should know better than to report in that uniform."

I didn't like the spotlight. I explained my Navy clothes were probably in a basement locker at my parents' St. Louis apartment.

"I'm not going to argue with you. The Navy store is open. Buy an outfit and be in proper uniform by muster tomorrow morning if you want to be an officer."

I couldn't believe this was happening in front of the officer candidates. I responded impulsively: "I'm not sure I want to be an officer."

I watched his face turn purple. Glaring at me, he shouted: "Where in the hell did you come from?"

I said, "Korea."

Dilemma at Newport

With his lips curled, nostrils flaring, he said, "We flew you over eight thousand miles and you are standing here telling me you're not sure you want to become an officer?" A murmur swept over the group. The commander threw up his hands in a gesture of futility. Pointing a finger at me he said, "I'll deal with you later."

After that exchange, I didn't hear another word he said. I was finished with the Navy.

We broke into smaller groups assigned to barracks, underwent a minor physical exam, and had the rest of the day to get squared away.

I asked the chief over our group who I could approach about my situation. He said I needed to go to the personnel office. I made an appointment for 0800 the next morning.

With a sly smile, the chief said I'd really teed off the commander. "I've never seen anything like that before."

I didn't go to bed that night. The commander was pissed, and so was I. My dad's words danced in my head that I should become a naval officer.

It was to be a long night.

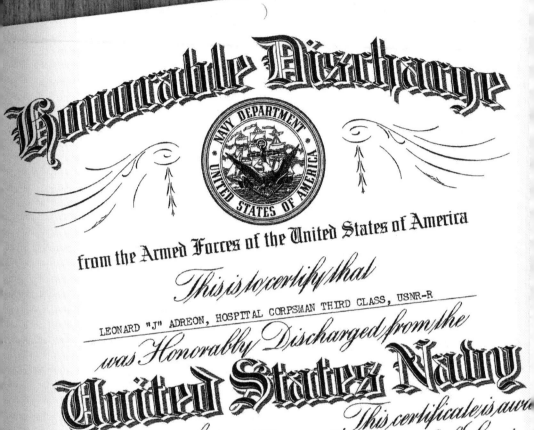

38

Final decision
Rhode Island, 1952

What should I do? I could take the course and become an officer, wear the handsome uniform and sail the world for four years. I could take the course and deliberately fail, avoiding both a return to Korea and extending my active duty. Or I could refuse the course and accept the consequences, whatever they might be.

The commander assumed that I knew in Korea I had only a few months to serve. He'd accused me of cowardly leaving my outfit in Korea. In doing so, he'd put the final seal on my decision.

The personnel office said I needed to write a letter to the Bureau of Naval Personnel explaining why I didn't want to attend the school. The letter would go to Washington, D.C., after being reviewed by the school's commander.

I spent hours on the letter. I emphasized that a key factor was the unreasonable time lapse from application to acceptance. I noted that I applied immediately after being recalled to active duty and detailed how I was fully qualified.

I delivered the letter to the personnel office around 1 p.m. Two hours later, the order came to report to the commander's office.

"This is bullshit," he said, waving the letter at me. "Adreon, you accepted these orders to escape from a combat zone. You're trying to pull a fast one on us."

Alone in his office, the language got rough between us. I said his comments in front of the class were unwarranted and were, in fact, stupid. I thanked him for making my decision easy because I didn't want to spend the next four years reporting to officers like him.

He ranted and raved and called me a "Chicken-shit SOB."

It was all I could do to not attack him, but I shut down and scowled. He finally calmed enough to say he had to forward my letter but was going to tell the bureau to ship me back to Korea. He then added, "I hope you get your ass shot off!"

I started to get out of my chair and he immediately stood up, shouting for me to sit down. "I'm not done with you yet."

I thought the veins in his neck might explode as he pounded his right fist into his left hand, saying that until the bureau responded, he'd have me assigned every dirty job on the base. "You'll have no privileges and no liberty. Now get the hell out of my office."

Final decision

He kept his word. I scrubbed floors, cleaned heads (toilets) and endured every other lousy detail. I derived some comfort from the chief and others taking my side. I made friends among the guys.

After thirty days, it became clear the Navy couldn't get me back to Korea. Even out of spite, the Navy wouldn't give a lowly corpsman special priority to prepare and travel to Korea for what would be a month or so.

I never saw the commander again, despite remaining at the school until I was released from active duty.

My military career was over.

39

Invisible wounds
Korea, 1951

The Navy took charges of cowardice seriously. But the accused were given a chance to explain themselves, if they could. Sometimes it took sensitivity, not normally associated with Marines, to get troops to talk.

I learned that at the battalion base after a brutal week at the 38th. With things unusually quiet, Doc Koz called me and Sammy and other corpsmen to a corner of the tent.

"We expect a quiet few days," he said, adding that the hospital, Easy Med, needed help from corpsmen. "Anyone willing to go?"

Sammy gave me the thumbs up. We volunteered with two others to drive a Jeep to the hospital, a few miles south. We got tossed around on the bumpy ride, which was otherwise uneventful.

As we approached the hospital, we heard the constant roar of motors as a parade of Bell copters landed and took off.

Marines rushed the wounded into the treatment areas. Departing copters carried more seriously wounded to hospital ships.

We reported to a chief warrant officer. He asked about our experience. Sammy, the senior corpsman of the group, went to major surgery, which involved full anesthesia. Two others went to minor surgery.

He asked if I could handle amputations. I told him I didn't feel qualified. "No one wants to work amputations," he said. To my relief, he assigned me to be available to whatever doctor needed help.

I covered many jobs over the next two days. I helped a doctor open up stomachs to stem bleeding. Or he removed shattered kidneys and spleens. I helped install chest-drainage tubes. I set up IV drips for saline solution, blood plasma, atropine and morphine.

On two occasions, I had to find a chaplain to give last rites to a dying Marine. I didn't know we had chaplains in Korea.

I delivered supplies to the surgery tents. I helped doctors remove arteries from a Marine who had died, placing the blood vessels in gallon jars filled with a solution. A new procedure used the arteries to sometimes save a leg or an arm.

On my last day at the field hospital, a doctor asked me to work with a psychiatrist on special cases. I didn't know there were psychiatrists in Korea.

One explained that if a Marine abandoned his post, in battle or otherwise, he received a psychological evaluation to decide if he needed medical treatment or a Captain's Mast hearing. The court-like hearing would decide if the Marine

Invisible wounds

deserved punishment.

The hospital devoted a tent to mental patients. Doctors had treated some for wounds such as from shrapnel or bullets. Others had no wounds.

The doctor quietly explained that fighting at the 38th traumatized some. That sometimes, it's easier for them to open up to a fellow Marine than to a shrink.

"I want to learn what happened to them," the doc explained. Whatever they could tell me would help. He suggested I ask why they thought they were in the hospital.

Most were 20 years old or younger. "You are older than they are," he said. "That might help."

I said I'd give it a try.

The doc brought me to a Marine private sitting in a crude wooden chair alongside a bunk. He just sat, not moving.

I told him I was from St. Louis, Missouri and wanted to help him feel better. He stared at me. I offered to shake his hand. He didn't move.

He was a good-looking kid with a round face, smooth, freckled skin, russet crew-cut hair and sad, droopy eyes. I walked to the kitchen and got us cups of red-colored juice. He took it and drank.

I said I couldn't help him if he wouldn't talk to me. He just stared.

I told the doctor. He shrugged, took me over to a Marine private first class in the next row of bunks—a tough-looking guy, scraggy face, unshaven, dark complexion, maybe Hispanic or Native American.

We started talking. "You a corpsman?" he asked.

I nodded, "Yeah."

"Told the doctor, I'm worn out. Wanna go home. Need to go home."

"How long you been here?"

He said six month that felt like six years. "I shot six gooks in a hole. Killed 'em all. They were just kids."

He squirmed, shook his head.

"Can't do it anymore."

He took a deep breath. Tears gathered in the corner of his eyes. "God will punish me. I'm goin' to hell. Ready to end it now."

He described standing on a hilltop, straight up, bullets flying all around, didn't duck, just stood. "I yelled at the gooks to kill me."

He described how his sergeant tackled him, threw him down. "I was screaming. I bit him, fought him. He and others knocked me down. Someone stuck a needle in me.

"Now I'm here, all fucked up."

I didn't know what to say, didn't have the words to console or reason with him. I told the doctor that I thought he needed a preacher, not a corpsman. "Adreon," the doc said, "what happened between you and him was good. He opened up, he somewhat grasps the problem. You helped."

Then the first private called me, "Doc, I wanna tell you somethin." I went to where he sat. His eyes filled with tears, his face stretched tight in anguish. He reached up, grabbed his head in his hands. He shook violently.

Invisible wounds

I sat on the bunk, watching. The shaking stopped. He looked at me. "Left our barricade to go take a crap. Came back. Joe, who had replaced me, had a hole in his neck. The three other guys at the barricade lay covered in blood. I had told Joe I would be right back. He told me, 'Be careful out there.'

Probably his last words."

Tears flowed down his cheeks. "Joe was a good guy, a good guy."

The doctor saw what was happening and came over. I said something like, "Not your fault, bullets flying everywhere, not your fault."

I moved away, realizing that not all the wounds of war come from bullets or shrapnel or bombs.

Some wounds don't bleed.

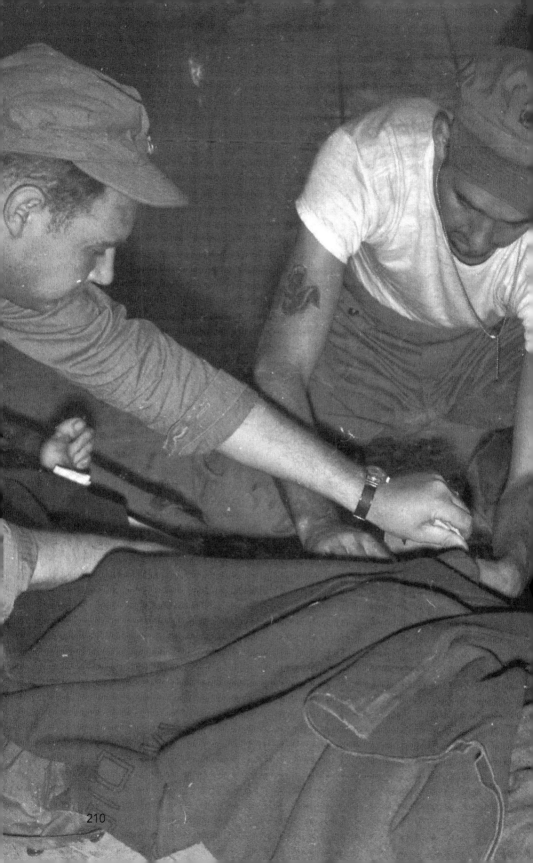

40

The diary
Korea, 1951

So I was swabbing the many toilet floors at the Naval Officer Candidate School, among the menial tasks assigned to me by the school's angry commander. The irony struck me: I'd gone from swabby to corpsman to Marine and back to swabby.

When tempted to feel sorry for myself, I remembered the diary—the sad story of another Marine's military journey. The memory of that Marine's words shouted that I should be OK with my Newport punishment.

It had been another wet, dreary day in the receiving tent, waiting with Doc Koz for the next stretcher. The flap opened, wind spraying drizzle as a stretcher came in with the limp body of a Marine.

Dr. Koz signaled me. "Adreon, I need to see the wound."

I grabbed large shears and ripped into the jacket, filled

with black, clotted blood. I next cut the Marine's shirt and undershirt. When I pulled up the undershirt, a thin pamphlet fell to the ground.

Hardened blood covered the spiral-bound booklet. I poked it with my shears and the brittle blood broke apart, revealing the single word, DIARY. I told Dr. Koz the Marine was ready.

The doctor checked his neck for a pulse, listened to his chest, and turned to say the Marine wouldn't make it. "Cover him and take him to the exit for transport."

The other corpsman and I moved the stretcher to the other end of the tent. Looking back, I saw the diary and carried it to his stretcher. The Marine had died.

The doctor checked him, closed his eyelids and recorded the time of death.

I asked Koz about the diary. He said I should put it on the stretcher, and his personal effects would go to his kin.

I sat on the ground next to the Marine and opened the diary. Inside, handwritten notes were scattered across lined pages.

I don't have it in front of me, but can remember clearly much of what was said. The first page read something like this:

Dad will try to do what you asked and keep a journal of my time in the Marines don't know why you want it no big deal, so here goes

Joined the Marines after high school cause I couldn't find a job,

The diary

probably because of my miserable high school record   it was 1950   there was no war   thought I'd look good in the uniform   would get duty in an embassy in some far off exciting place

   A few lines down came a second entry that was something like:

   Parris Island, South Carolina   Marine Boot Camp   did ok   no discipline problems   unusual for me   the DI worked us hard   best shape of my life   they cut off my long hair   like the buzz cut   spent about 9 months   transferred to Camp Pendleton, California.

   His writing was reasonably legible, written in pencil and scribbled across the page, mostly ignoring the lines.

Camp Pendleton   Advanced training in machine guns   like firing the guns   thought it was a waste because where and when would I fire em

bad news   war in Korea   where the hell is Korea   fast track war training at Pendleton   1st Marine Division

spring 1951   jammed together with many others on a ship named after some general

   miserable conditions   hot and crowded   can't wait to get off the ship   seasick half the time   throwing up   couldn't eat the shit they served us

arrived Pusan, Korea   what a shitty place   smells like a sewer

what a mess   fucked up by the war   to take a crap we squat like the gooks over a hole in the ground   everything is beat up and filthy

a screwed up war   we crawl up a hill gooks shooting at us   I'm pretty damn good on the machine gun   kill many gooks but they keep comin   stupid motherfuckers never stop   can't kill em fast enough   we take a hill   lose a hill   take it again getting nowhere FUCK FUCK FUCK   how many times do I have to do this   like anything else do it too much it'll get you

I'm exhausted   I'd walk away if I could   can't   if the gooks don't get me   the Marines will   I'm stuck   kill enough and maybe they'll make peace   I've killed plenty

there are peace talks somewhere nearby

have a bad feeling   scared   why am I writing all this shit   not going to write any more

enough   if I make it home I'll bring this journal home   don't know why but I will

I remember he skipped some pages, leaving them blank. Near the end of the diary came a clear message:

if I die in this fuckin' awful place don't want this journal sent home whoever finds it   burn it   my dad must never see it   don't want him to feel bad cause he pushed me out of the house into the Marine Corps

maybe someone will think I did something right

maybe I did

The diary

I showed the last page to Koz. He looked at me and said I could put it with the Marine's body to be sent home, or burn it as he asked.

"Adreon, It's your call."

I burned it.

41

Vacationing home
Missouri, 1952

The Marine kept a diary, but like so many warriors coming home, didn't really want to share the memories. I understood, and explained that to my family when I finally saw them again.

In my Marine uniform with duffle hoisted, I'd walked away from the school in Newport—never to find myself on another military base. To paraphrase Yogi Berra, when it's over, it's over.

My pay in Korea had accumulated, putting money in my pocket. I felt rich and reckless. I could go wherever I wanted.

I wanted a car, never having owned one. At a used lot in Newport, I bought an ugly green 1948 Chevrolet Sports Coupe for $425. I didn't care that I hated the color. It was *my* ugly car.

I also wanted a vacation and decided the winter logic was to drive to Florida. I'd never been, and saw myself flaking out on a beach. A sense of freedom drove me. No one was telling me where to be and what to do.

Driving through a place called Hollywood, Florida, I heard a siren and saw flashing lights behind me.

The policeman came to my window. I handed over my Missouri license, pleasantly surprised it hadn't expired. The cop said I was going 55 in a 40 mile-per-hour zone. "I'll have to take you into the station."

I appealed to his patriotic spirit, saying I was just back from Korea and anxious to see my mom and dad in Florida. I flashed the Korea ribbons on my Marine uniform. "Can't you give me a warning?"

I learned men returning from Korea would get nothing special. His so-what attitude told me how the war was perceived in the States. "You were speeding," he said, shaking his head. "I'll give you a ticket, though I should bring you in since you're from out of state."

Maybe he should've. I never paid the ticket. I later got a notice that Hollywood, Florida, had issued a warrant for my arrest. As far as I know, I'm still a wanted man. Somehow, I don't feel guilty.

I took time to call and have a long talk with Dad. Turns out he was fine with choosing against the school. Apparently, his concern was that I'd be sent back to Korea.

I found a little motel just outside Miami located right on the beach. I bought a swimsuit and let the sun beat down,

Vacationing home

splashing a bit in the ocean. Bored after a few days, I drove across the Everglades to Florida's west coast.

On the way, I took a hovercraft ride across the swamps. After a few days on the sparkling white sand beaches of the Gulf of Mexico, I grew restless again.

Decided that New Orleans was a place I should see, zipping over Highway 90 to treat myself to a French Quarter hotel. I did the bar scene on Bourbon Street, watched the shows and met local lovelies. I drank too much, partied too much, spent too much and lost too much of my self control.

It was time to drive north, to begin the quest for the future I'd chosen.

If I doubted my decision, I only had to picture the school's commander, resplendent in his Navy uniform, to know that was not for me.

Mom, Dad and my brother, Mert, gave me a wonderful welcome in St. Louis. They wanted to know all about my experiences in Korea, saying my letters had been vague about what was happening.

Mert found a letter I had written: "I'm in the rear with my gear and a beer and glad to be here." I apparently thought that was clever.

They understood when I explained that a group of us had decided to move on and not reflect on the war.

My family and I never talked about it again.

42

Another ending
Korea, winter 1951/1952

Our drill instructor at Pendleton told us not to get too chummy with our fellow Marines in Korea. He didn't detail why. He simply said it was a bad idea. We understood.

But buddies we became. I found one in the rec tent, where I'd gone for a drink on a snowy day. My fellow platoon corpsman, Sammy, sat at a table alone so I joined him, beer in hand. He smiled as he sipped his.

Until that day, I didn't know much about Sammy. I knew this was his second tour in the Navy and he'd reached the rank of Hospital Corpsman 1rd Class, making him our company's senior corpsman.

He said he joined the Navy after high school and asked for the medical corps. His uncle was a lab technician and told him medicine offered good jobs, that being a navy corpsman would be great on his resume.

Sammy grew up in Brooklyn or the Bronx. He said his schools had numbers, not names like in St. Louis. He liked sports and played on his high school basketball team. Strong and athletic, Sammy was just short of 6 feet tall, with reddish brown hair and an abundance of freckles.

He had a ready smile. Sammy spoke softly even in the most stressful of circumstances. He said his dad was a moderately successful salesman at a large discount department store. Sammy said this was his last tour in the Navy, with less than a year left.

Then came another hill on a frigid, snow-filled day. We had made it up with fewer casualties than usual. Our bombers and artillery had blasted the hilltop to suppress any Chinese opposition.

Sammy, I and other corpsmen worked the hilltop, helping load wounded Marines on stretchers for transport to the forward aid station. We next checked fallen Chinese, treating those alive and marking those to be stacked with other Chinese bodies on the hill's north side.

Sammy and I worked in tandem. He'd examine a body, feel for a pulse, and shout for me to tag it. I worked behind him in this gruesome work for about two hours when, through the falling snow, I saw him approach a Chinese rifleman face down on the wet ground.

Another ending

Sammy brushed the snow off the body and reached under to turn him over. A sudden flash of light, and an explosion shook the hilltop, leaving a cloud of billowing smoke. When the air cleared I couldn't see Sammy or the fallen Chinese.

I yelled for help and rushed with several Marines to find Sammy's battered and bloody body. He had no chance. Sammy fell victim to a booby-trap grenade left by the retreating Chinese.

Sammy tragically died doing what he'd always done: trying to help the wounded, whether Marines or the enemy.

We'd lost our best corpsman. The Marines lost a man who'd saved many others. Sammy was my mentor. He took over when I couldn't bring myself to try a tracheotomy. He set an example with his steady and compassionate approach to his duties.

I crawled into the foxhole that Sammy and I'd planned to share. I buried myself in the sleeping bag and closed my eyes. I found it hard to sleep, seeing images of Sammy and me at the barricade where a direct hit had killed a group of dug-in Marines, of having a beer together at the rec tent, of Sammy leading me through the mud and crud of hills and valleys.

After a long night, a sliver of light penetrated the cloud cover. The snow had stopped. I unzipped the bag and climbed out of the hole. It was strangely quiet.

I walked to the edge of the hilltop, intrigued by the sight below. It was as if a white comforter had covered the hillside, in almost ethereal serenity.

I was alone, a solitary figure on the hilltop. A tranquil moment amid a frantic war.

History and Perspective

Epilogue
Missouri, 2016

Only now, more than 60 years after returning home, have I allowed myself to think, talk and write about my time in Korea. When I came home in 1952, I detected little interest in the war. In those years, there were no 24/7 news channels amid the fuzzy little pictures displayed on TVs. Most people got their news from radio and newspapers.

They called it the Forgotten War. Of course, it is forgotten. The years have dulled our memories. Not many of us around any more. My memory consists mostly of faces, people, tears, anxiety, tension, noise, confusion, blood, mud and crud.

Upon arriving in Korea, I learned that the war had raged from Pusan on the South to Pyongyang on the North and had settled in the area of the 38th Parallel. We no longer fought for territory. It wasn't even about winning. I was stunned when our commander said our purpose was to dominate the high ground and kill and maim as many of the enemy as possible. The goal had narrowed to forcing the Chinese and North Koreans to agree to a ceasefire.

Looking back, I've tried to understand my feelings as a 24 year old in this kill-or-maim war. How did I feel while assaulting the enemy, lifting my carbine, holding the trigger down, sending 30 potentially deadly rounds at the enemy? How did I feel when I walked among the bodies of the dead Chinese? Did any of my bullets kill? Does it matter?

How did I feel treating wounded Marines, knowing that in many cases, their quality of life was forever diminished? Or when I helped load dead Marines onto trucks for their long sad trip home?

For the most part, they were kids in their teens or early 20's. Their future was impaired or gone. I felt a deep sadness. I felt sick to my stomach. I had to be careful not to let anyone see how I felt. We were tough. We were Marines.

After multiple encounters, those feelings diminished. Our duties became routine. I was a corpsman. My job was to treat the wounded. I moved from foxhole to barricades and on the hillsides to find the wounded and dead. All of us corpsmen did our job understanding that if the Marines failed, our bodies would be lying on the ground.

I watched a Marine Corsair fly low and spray a Chinese battalion with relentless fire. He killed a dozen or more on one run. How did he feel when the men fell? Elation, success, a surge of power, grandeur, omnipotence? Did he even feel good? I didn't know then and I don't know now.

Epilogue

Looking into one foxhole, I saw four Chinese still holding their burp guns, leaning against a dirt bank, each staring with unseeing eyes at the sky. Their war was over. Somewhere in China, a mother, father, sister or brother waited for their return. They would not know what happened to their loved one.

In those moments, I felt the futility of what we were doing. However, we had no choice. We would continue to kill and maim whenever and however we could.

One of my Marine buddies saw me treat a wounded Chinese. He asked why I helped him when his fellow soldiers had left him to die. I told him that he was a human being and that without treatment he would die. I watched the Marine scoff, shake his head, and walk away. He didn't get it. Such was the attitude of many in that war.

The war diminished the value of a life. The lists of dead and wounded became mere numbers. We measured success by how many more we killed than we lost. It sickened me to hear a report that, on a given day, the Marines lost only 12 men, while the enemy lost more than twice that many. That's good news?

I felt then and I feel now that no one won. We all lost by perpetuating a war. I don't think it matters if it was World War II or Korea or any other war. The destruction turns everyone into a loser. I am sorry for all those damaged by the war. To lose a son or daughter to combat has to be terrible.

I'm lucky to be here writing about the feelings of war. In the middle of a battle, there is no time to feel. I think that is worth repeating. Amid a war's fury, there is no time to feel anything. Only later can we reflect on the tragic sadness.

I have written these pages as a tribute to those who didn't come back and to all the lives damaged. I write to present a perspective on war, its brutality and its misery, with the hope that anyone who reads my words will know that war is the worst way to solve disputes.

I'm glad to have finished the task of writing about my experiences in this war. I'm not certain that I remembered details precisely. I'm sure there is much that I couldn't or didn't want to recall.

My daughter, Linda Morgan, visited the Korean War Veterans Memorial in Washington D. C. and sent pictures. She felt good about visiting the memorial. I've not been there.

In photos, I've seen that the soldiers, Marines, airmen and sailors are depicted as realistic figures wearing parkas amid the worst winter conditions. I arrived in Korea in the spring of 1951 and left before the coldest months of 1951/52. I didn't wear my parka because I got by without it. It tended to slow me down.

I am pleased that, finally, the Korean War was recognized and memorialized for the public to see.

I am proud of the United States Marine Corps. I am proud I was a corpsman with the First Marine Division. I was lucky. One hundred and eight of my fellow corpsmen were killed in the three-year war. Five corpsmen serving in Korea, four of whom were killed in action, were awarded the nation's highest military honor, the Congressional Medal of Honor.

Epilogue

I tried my best to live up to the high standards of the Marine Corps. Although I doubt that I appreciated it at the time, the Marines who trained us at Camp Pendleton knew how to instill an esprit de corps that hasn't diminished. I still tear up when the Marine Corps Hymn is played on Memorial Day and Veterans Day.

Poems

THE FLAMES OF WAR
Leonard Adreon

In a war you kill the enemy
You are trained to destroy life

We crawl up the hill to stop
a killer machine gun in a bunker
lift the massive weapons
pull the triggers of death.
Flames leap from black barrels
Spew fiery destruction
sears the bunker

He runs out
flesh burned black
falling, twisting, rolling
screaming, choking, dying
A kid, just a kid

In a quiet Chinese village
a child is born
given life and hope
love and nourishment,

A kind good gentle boy
He dashes, tumbles, laughs
radiates joy to delight
parents and others,

Circumstances change
Conflict, turmoil
The child grows up
to fight for "a cause".
On a hill, trapped in a bunker
Stop the enemy, fire away
Do your job, for country
flag and honor.

No way out
Helpless against the fury of the flames
Can't see, eyes on fire,
Unbearable heat
scorches the skin, singes hair
body burning, gyrating,
inhaling flames, can't breathe,
The acrid odor of burnt flesh.
Pain stops, movement ends.

Casket closed
Charred remains inside,
Eighteen years, so loved,
A short brave life.

Vacant words at the grave
from those who sent him to die.

Another young man's life
ends in the flames of war.

THE PROUD BATTERED FLAG
Leonard Adreon

The killing is over
The hill quiet
No bugles, whistles, screaming shouts
No shell blasts, burp gun staccato
Only the sound of the wind
reshuffling the dreary dusty debris

The hill with no name
Scarred burnt tree trunks
Blackened earth
Shell pitted craters
Colorless shapeless
waste filled gullies
Black grey dirty brown

The aroma of battle lingers
Fetid odor of decay
Acrid stench of charred flesh
Remnants of arms legs eyes
buried below the grey residue

Heavy black clouds hover
A sliver of an opening
A ray of sunlight bursts through
Shimmers like a spotlight
illuminates the hilltop
focuses of the remnants of
a sad scarred flag
mounted on a crooked pole

Stars on blue field
Red and white stripes
Tattered ragged edges
hanging limp on the pole

A touch of wind
Flag unfurls in
the filtered sunlight
Brightness out of darkness
A sparkling beam of light
on the proud battered flag
atop the ghastly hill

A tribute to those
whose blood was splattered
so that the flag can shine
adding a color of hope
to the hill of misery.

SERGEANT JIMMY
Leonard Adreon

On a hill with no name
seven thousand miles from home
Marine Sergeant Jimmy leads his platoon
up a rocky slope
through heavy soaked air
shadowed visibility
his M1 at the ready.

Flashes of light from above
vibration of explosions
staccato sounds of guns
bullets splaying into boulders.

Jimmy pulls the pin
hurls the grenade
the blast, bodies fly
one lone soldier staggers out
fires as he falls on soggy earth
Jimmy clutches his chest
face down in the mud
corpsman at his side
hang on, hang on
bleeding stops, signs ok.

Sergeant Jimmy looks up
Muffled conversations
the Doctor working intensely
hands moving fast
 push, pull, stretch

Eyes clouded, face contorted
he sees his Mom, Dad, Sisters
reaches up to touch smiling faces
A party, bright lights, singing, laughing
the banner,   GOOD LUCK
COME BACK SOON.

Sergeant Jimmy on his way home
seven thousand miles
The plane lands
to family and friends who wait.

A wooden box, flag draped
Sergeant Jimmy
twenty- two years old
Marines salute
His journey over.

Let every day be a
a day to remember
to honor, to give thanks
to Sergeant Jimmy and all those
who gave up a life
 a limb, an eye or more.

For all of us

For each of us.

Dedicated to my friend,
James Henry Marshall

SALUTE THEM, HONOR THEM, REMEMBER THEM
Leonard Adreon

They died in the trenches of World War Two
in the wet, mud, slime, blood
in distant lands to the East, to the West

They died in the foxholes or on a mountain
in oppressive heat and numbing cold
in the rice-paddy filled landscape of Korea

They died in a lost-cause war
unsupported by people at home
unappreciated for their sacrifice in Vietnam

They died in the sandy desolation of Iraq
destroyed by a hidden device called an IED
planted by vicious unseen enemies

They died on the rocks and crevices of Afghanistan
where every step may be the last

World War Two survivors are sparse in number
Soon there will be no more
Korea is lost in the yellowing pages of history

Veterans Hospitals overflow with the tragic victims
destined to be only a memory

So many died, lives shattered
by an early death
 or the damages of war
Torn battered bodies and broken minds

Death surrounds us still
In the debris that once was Syria
In the remnants of Afghanistan

Blood even flows in peaceful
places where people gather to pray
work, shop, learn or simply come together

They gave up their futures
so we can be here today
to treasure each moment

The story continues

2017

Many people said we lost the war. After all, when the war started on June 25, 1950, there were two Koreas divided at the 38th Parallel. When the killing stopped on July 27th, 1953, two Koreas remained divided at the 38th Parallel. President Syngman Rhee did not realize his goal of one democratic Korea.

The maps on the following pages tell the story of the conflict.

What if we hadn't fought the war? Kim Jong-un undoubtedly would rule one Korea. The 50 million people of South Korea would be living in misery like the sad people of North Korea.

South Korea thrives today as a free nation. South Koreans are a kind, compassionate people who survived a brutal

Japanese occupation and a devastating invasion by North Korea, compounded by China's intervention.

The war did not end. Only a ceasefire, called an armistice, emerged in 1953. In 2009, the North Koreans repudiated that agreement. Then four years later, North Korea said it had scrapped all non-aggression pacts with South Korea.

Today, the Demilitarized Zone (DMZ) near the 38th Parallel is the most heavily defended national border in the world. About 25,000 United States service members are stationed in Korea. After all these years, the Korean Peninsula seems poised to resume the war that never ended.

The costs of war

The United States incurred more than one half of its Korean War casualties during the two years and 17 days of peace talks.

5.7 million active as U.S. Servicemembers worldwide (1950-1953)

1.8 million served in Korea; of those:

103,284 were wounded

33,739 died on the battlefield **+ 2,835** died from other causes

For every 50 serving in Korea:

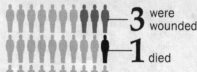

3 were wounded
1 died

Lasting impact

7,799 missing in action

2.3 million living veterans

Sources: Department of Veterans Affairs, Defense POW/MIA Accounting Agency; all figures as of 2016

A brief history of the Korean War.

KOREA DIVIDED IN WWII

July 1945: Potsdam Conference
The United States and Soviet Union agree to divide Korea at the 38th Parallel – Soviet Union in the north, United States in the south.

Aug. 15, 1945: Japanese surrender marks the end of WWII.

1947: In March, President Truman declares The Truman Doctrine pledging assistance to any nation threatened by Communism. American forces begin departure from Korea later that year.

1948: Syngman Rhee is elected first President of South Korea. He claims sovereignty over all of Korea. In response, Kim Il-Sung also proclaims sovereignty over the peninsula.

NORTH KOREA ATTACKS

May 1950: Kim Il-Sung meets with Joseph Stalin in Moscow and gets his approval to invade the south.

June 25, 1950: North Korea invades South Korea. Rhee orders his military to eliminate those he believes threaten his regime. 100,000 are executed in the "summer of terror."

June 27, 1950: The United Nations and the United States condemn North Korea for its action. President Truman commits U.S. forces to the conflict.

June 28, 1950: North Korea captures Seoul, the capital of South Korea.

Aug. 4, 1950: U.S. Forces land at Inchon to open a new front.

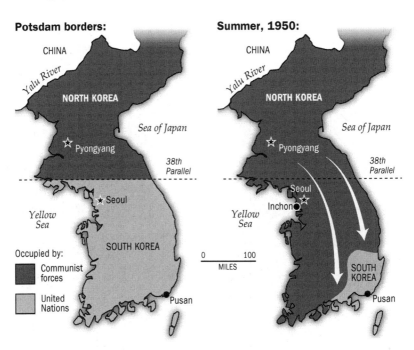

History and perspective

MACARTHUR PUSHES BACK

Sept. 27, 1950: President Truman authorizes an advance into North Korea beyond the 38th Parallel.

Oct. 15, 1950: President Truman meets with General MacArthur on Wake Island. MacArthur tells Truman that it is his evaluation that the Chinese will not enter the conflict.

Oct. 20, 1950: United States forces reach Pyongyang, the capital of North Korea and victory seems in sight.

November 1950: China enters the war, sending hundreds of thousand of troops across the Yalu River.

STALEMATE AT THE 38TH

Spring, 1951: Korean War reaches a stalemate near the 38th Parallel. *Author Leonard Adreon arrives in Korea.*

April 1951: President Truman fires General MacArthur.

June 10, 1951: Peace talks begin

November 4, 1952: Dwight D. Eisenhower is elected U.S. President, vowing to end the war in Korea.

July 27, 1953: Armistice signed at Panmunjom ends conflict. No peace treaty is negotiated.

Fall, 1950:

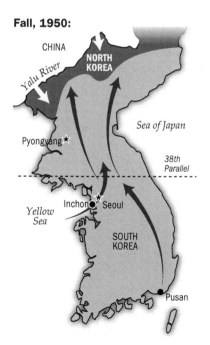

1953 Armistice:

Final observations
St. Louis, Mo. 2020

Since this book was first published in 2017, I have received many questions from people who have read my book. I thought it might be worthwhile to answer some of these questions. Also, because 68 years have passed since my Korean experience, I believe my perspective might be of interest.

First let me try to answer some of the questions.

What did you eat while in combat on the hills or at the base?

I chuckled that some readers are interested in our meals. At the base we ate in a mess hall and had a variety of meals prepared by competent cooks. We had hot meals and the food was OK. In the field, we mostly existed on C Rations which were cans of food adequate for our nourishment. These cans had a key that we removed to open the sealed can. I remember a variety, like franks and beans, beef stew with vegetables, ham and lima beans, chopped eggs and ham, and more. I thought the food was surprisingly good, especially when we could build a fire and heat it up. Also available were packets of cookies, crackers, gum, powdered milk, coffee, cigarettes and matches.

When you were in a foxhole on a hilltop, how did you relieve yourself?

That could be dangerous. If the enemy was lobbing mortars at the hilltop, we had to leave the foxhole, run to a remote place, relieve ourselves and using a little shovel we

Final observations

carried in our backpacks, cover over what we did. I clearly hesitated to leave the foxhole on many occasions because I knew the shrapnel was flying. We moved fast and became adept at timing the shelling to avoid the mortars.

Sounds like you carried a lot of stuff going up a hill. What was it all?

On my web belt, I usually had two med kits fully loaded. I also carried more on my belt, unlike some corpsmen, including a holstered .45-caliber pistol. That alone probably weighed more than three pounds. I wore a bandolier that held cartridges for the .45 and 30-round clips for my M1 Carbine rifle, which was slung across my shoulder. I also carried a few grenades, so I was pretty loaded. We all carried backpacks with changes of clothing, sleeping bags, a shovel and some other items.

How did you get clean after crawling up a hill sometimes in wet muddy conditions?

Often, after securing the hill, there was a small creek running somewhere or a hole with water in it. We would sometimes take what I called a Korean Shower. I would stand in the water, use my helmet to scoop some up and pour it over myself. The ugly thing was that the water was often very dirty. I never knew what crud I was pouring. At other times, we had water that was hauled up the hill that, in limited quantities, we could use to wash ourselves. I do not think I ever felt clean at the 38th.

You were a navy corpsman serving with the Marines. What was the relationship between you and the Marine riflemen and officers? Did you have a red cross on your uniform or helmet or some other identification to show you were a medic?

My rank as a Navy petty officer third-class was probably the equivalent of a Marine corporal. In combat, corpsmen did not want to stand out because the enemy would target them. I was dressed like any other corporal except the insignia on my upper sleeve was a medical symbol called a Caduceus (looks like two snakes winding around a winged staff). Don't know what snakes have to do with medicine.

I admired and respected the Marines with whom I served. I am glad to say that the Marines were respectful of us corpsmen. They knew that we would risk our lives to help them if they were wounded. We knew they would do all they could to protect us. I observed that any rank in combat had no meaning except to identify who was giving the orders. The lieutenant, the sergeant and the rest of us were all in this together. Despite the stress of the situation, we were a cohesive team.

You said in the book that your mission was to kill and maim as many of the enemy as possible to force the Chinese leaders to negotiate an end to the war. However, you gave first aid to Chinese wounded. Why didn't you let them bleed out and die? Did you ever consider actually causing them to die?

I can't speak for all corpsmen or Marines. I never had a desire to let a wounded man die or to do anything that would hasten his death. These were young men doing their duty

Final observations

just as we were doing ours. Many of the Chinese soldiers were teen-age kids. After treatment, the Chinese became prisoners of war. I didn't hate them. I felt compassion for them. I'm sure that some of the Marines and, maybe, some corpmen, felt differently and would sometimes even shoot a wounded enemy soldier.

Several people said that I did not adequately describe how I felt about what was happening or what had happened.

I think that is a valid observation. There is a fury in a combat situation that doesn't allow for participants to reflect on what is happening. To me, we just did what we had to do. It was all about trying to complete a mission. It was also about survival.

I am horrified that the world continues to fail to solve problems in a peaceful manner. At age 25, I killed young Chinese kids. I had no choice. Looking into the face of a dead 18-year-old soldier is one of the saddest things I have had to do.

I am in the twilight of my life. I have shared what I know about that war to build awareness, to present a realistic picture of a ground war and to honor those who served, as well as those who died or were wounded in that miserable, 37-month war.

The Korean Dilemma

I have been asked numerous times my opinion of the present circumstances in Korea. My observation and opinion follows:

Brutal killing is still happening in many places in the world. It feels like we are always on the brink of another war. We have something like 28,000 troops in Korea today. My experience all those years ago tells me that we should never fight another ground war on that peninsula. It is my opinion that prosperous South Korea (population about 51 million), with some military equipment from the United States, should be able to defend itself.

It concerns me that, so far, we have been unable to reach an accord with North Korea and stop Kim Jong-un's quest for an intercontinental nuclear missile capability.

He rules over twenty-five and one-half million impoverished and miserable people. He has threatened the world that he will strike the United States, Japan, South Korea and Australia if he feels they will attack him. Another dictator threatened the use of weapons of mass destruction (that he didn't have) which cost him his country and his life. Kim Jong-un should know this. He should realize that the surest way for him to lose his country and, probably his life, is to continue his threat. The motivation ought to be there to cause him to make a deal that will economically benefit his people in exchange for giving up his nuclear intentions.

Final observations

We must find a way to assure him that after he dismantles his nuclear capability, he can trust the United States to not reinstate sanctions or discontinue the economic aid that will be essential to making a binding agreement.. We must be assured via inspections that he will not resume his efforts to become a nuclear power.

Although it will be hard to achieve, my hope is that enough mutual trust between the parties can be developed so an agreement can be reached and Korea, at last, will have a stable peace. It's way past due for a peace treaty.

About the author

Etched in glass of the prestigious Cornerstone Award presented to Leonard Adreon are the words, "For his dedication and devotion to the Clayton Community." Those words capture the essence of Adreon's life after Korea.

He spent 36 years as the executive vice president of The Siteman Organization, a real estate management and development company, based in the St. Louis suburb of Clayton, Mo.

In 1979, he was elected president of the Building Owners and Managers Association International in Washington D. C., which represents the office building industry in the United States and across the globe. He represented the industry before a number of Senate and House committees, and earned a citation from the General Services Administration for advice on leasing and managing facilities throughout the world.

A highlight was meeting President Ronald Reagan and working with his chairman of the Council of Economic Advisors, Murray Weidenbaum.

St. Louis city and county leaders appointed Adreon to numerous committees and commissions serving his community. Adreon also took a leadership role in several major charities devoted to the welfare of children.

Upon his retirement from The Siteman Organization, he worked for two decades as a consultant, real estate broker, arbitrator and mediator.

Today, Adreon volunteers as a facilitator of writing classes at the Lifelong Learning Institute of Washington University in St. Louis. It is that work that encouraged him to tell his own story.

Adreon met his wife, Audrey, a year after his return from Korea. They have three daughters and six grandchildren.

Made in the USA
Columbia, SC
09 October 2022